Scripting
THE LIFE
YOU WANT

"Like a beautiful piece of art, you can create and design your own life. *Scripting the Life You Want* is a powerful step toward manifesting a beautiful life journey for yourself. There's tremendous power in words. *Scripting the Life You Want* will guide you toward changing the way you think, the way you speak, and change your life in the process. This book is the first step in writing the script to a beautiful life story—living and loving it!"

BRIAN BALTHAZAR, NATIONAL TELEVISION HOST,
FORMER CO-EXECUTIVE PRODUCER OF *THE VIEW*, AND
PAST EXECUTIVE PRODUCER OF
THE TODAY SHOW AND *HOUSE HUNTERS*

"We all know what we should do every day to set goals, and this book, with all of Royce's passionate encouragement, actually makes you want to do it! Royce has absolutely nailed explaining how we can go for what we want in life without rigidity, demanding that life bend to our will. It's about simply letting our creative mind work for us when we're dreaming of what kind of life we want and it can be done with easy-to-do, fun writing exercises. This book is spiritual in the best of ways because it's full of spirited advice from deep within the human spirit."

JEN KIRKMAN, COMEDIAN AND NEW YORK TIMES
BESTSELLING AUTHOR OF *I CAN BARELY TAKE CARE OF MYSELF*

"*Scripting the Life You Want* is an irresistible handbook for manifesting your dreams! Royce is an engaging, fun, and motivating guide, helping you go from where you are to where you want to be."

JOEL FOTINOS, COAUTHOR OF
THE THINK AND GROW RICH WORKBOOK

"Royce Christyn has pulled off the impossible . . . he's written an instruction manual that you cannot put down. It's riveting, touching, engaging, and oftentimes laugh-out-loud funny! Oh, and if you're an old hat at manifesting, or you think the whole Law of Attraction is nonsense but your curiosity has gotten the better of you, this book is for you! Royce has somehow managed to make the whole journey relatable, doable, and, dare I say, practical. No matter what, you'll enjoy his engaging stories and the way in which he tells them, and who knows, you just might get your wish in the process."

ORFEH, SINGER, SONGWRITER, AND
TONY-NOMINATED BROADWAY STAR OF *LEGALLY BLONDE*

"Royce illustrates the leading-edge concepts related to manifestation and the Law of Attraction into a simple, elegant masterpiece that provides the reader with a simple tool to manifest desires into reality. Truly magnificent."

AMY WAUCHOPE, CREATOR OF THE
YOUTUBE CHANNEL STARSEED 11:11

"This book is an invaluable resource for dreamers everywhere. Royce gives the reader a true how-to guide for how to manifest your goals into reality. This book is going to help people live their best lives."

TOM D'ANGORA, THREE-TIME DRAMA DESK–NOMINATED AND
OFF-BROADWAY ALLIANCE AWARD–WINNING
NEW YORK–BASED FILM AND THEATRICAL PRODUCER

"Want it. Believe it. Make it happen. Royce's simple technique will help you be the hero of your own story for the rest of your life. Wonderfully affirming and precisely what the world needs."

EMMA KENNEDY, AWARD-WINNING ACTRESS, WRITER,
AND AUTHOR OF *THE THINGS WE LEFT UNSAID*

Scripting
THE LIFE
YOU WANT

Manifest Your Dreams
with Just Pen and Paper

ROYCE CHRISTYN

Inner Traditions
Rochester, Vermont

Inner Traditions
One Park Street
Rochester, Vermont 05767
www.InnerTraditions.com

Text stock is SFI certified

Cataloging-in-Publication Data for this title is available from the Library of Congress

ISBN 978-1-64411-019-5 (print)
ISBN 978-1-64411-020-1 (ebook)

Printed and bound in the United States by Lake Book Manufacturing, Inc.
The text stock is SFI certified. The Sustainable Forestry Initiative® program
promotes sustainable forest management.

10 9 8 7 6 5 4 3 2 1

Text design and layout by Virginia Scott Bowman
This book was typeset in Garamond Premier Pro and Avenir with Harmon used as
the display typeface

Because hyperlinks do not always remain viable, URLs do not appear in the
resources, notes, or bibliographic entries. Instead the names of the websites where
this information may be found are provided.

To send correspondence to the author of this book, mail a first-class letter to the
author c/o Inner Traditions • Bear & Company, One Park Street, Rochester, VT
05767, and we will forward the communication, or contact the author directly at
roycechristyn.com.

First, I dedicate this book to all of the powerful and incredible women in the world. Regardless of whether we have had a long relationship (like my mother, Neva; my sisters Kira, Nancy, and Tiffany; my mother-in-law, Jane Hemus; my three best friends, Sara Galliano, Dr. Dena Grayson, and Kirsten Godshalk; my grandmothers Helen and Catherine; and my brilliant aunts Carol, Denise, Stephanie, Sharon, and Betty) or you are someone who has greatly inspired me in life (such as Lynn Grabhorn, Ellen DeGeneres, Oprah Winfrey, Anne Frank, Gayle King, Hillary Clinton, Esther Hicks, Eileen Caddy, Madonna, and the incredible Mel Robbins), the world is a better place because of your wisdom, power, and contributions. It is through your inspiration and example that I am who I am today. I am forever grateful to each of you, plus the hundreds more I haven't cited here by name, and the millions more I have yet to meet.

Second, I dedicate this book to the love of my life, Solly Hemus, and you, reader, who, as my hero Lynn Grabhorn once wrote, "finally . . . maybe . . . possibly . . . believes they have the right to perpetual happiness, beginning now."

Contents

The Power of One Simple Exercise

Mitch Horowitz

FOR YEARS I'VE BEEN ENCHANTED with a little pamphlet from the 1920s called *It Works*. You may know it. The author, who identified himself only as R. H. J. (he was a Chicago sales executive named Roy Herbert Jarrett), prescribed the following process for attaining the things you want in life: (1) write down your desires, (2) think of your list constantly, and (3) remain silent, telling no one what you're doing. Then give thanks when your wishes arrive.

I count myself among the generations of readers who found Roy's twenty-eight-page pamphlet too good to be true. Except for one nagging fact: it is true. I've written about Roy, his methods, and why they work (or seem to) for years. They've never been matched. Until now.

Royce Christyn—an actor, writer, director, and lifelong metaphysical seeker—gave me an exercise one day that was just offbeat enough, and just appealing enough, to try. I never could have imagined how much Royce's exercise would come to mean to me. And how quickly its effectiveness would be felt.

It happened this way: Royce and his partner, Solly, were treating me to a day trip to Disneyland—I had never visited the Magic Kingdom and was eager to squeeze as much into our few hours as possible. I had to return to LA that evening. It was a hot fall day, and the place was packed, shoulder to shoulder. Yet we whisked through lines, rode a popular ride twice, and covered the park almost to the extent of seeing and doing everything we wanted to. We were back on the road by 5:00 p.m. It was weird, improbable, and altogether true. (We've got pictures to prove it.)

During this whirlwind trip, Royce described to me a method of "scripting" out one's day, which he and Solly had been using. In its simplicity, I found it similar to Roy Jarrett's approach, but what Royce described was more vivid, timely, and detailed. And, above all, it proved effective. More than effective—uncanny.

As you will discover in this powerful, concise book, Royce's scripting method requires writing out your idealized day first thing in the morning, as if it already occurred. Then at night, just before bed, you write out your day once more, as you actually lived it. Over time the congruency between the two passages will emerge. That has been my experience. It has been jarring, wonderful, productive, and surprising. (As you'll see, Royce also provides a more long-term form of scripting in the book.)

Shortly after our Disney trip, Royce sent me two pages from Solly's journal, which reflected on our day: the idealized version was written in the morning (at early dawn), and the forensic version was written that night, following the day's events. Let me state this plainly: except for one detail, involving a gift I bought them at the park, the two passages are factually interchangeable. Improbable—and real.

I have been criticized for espousing a certain position about New Thought, but I will repeat it here because it comes from the heart, and it will help you understand my enthusiasm for Royce's method. In interviews I am open to virtually any question; nothing is off the table. There is one question, however, with which I struggle: "What new voices in New Thought excite you?" My answer: "Almost none." There are far too many metaphysical voices—both famous and unknown—who offer catechism, vagueness, and retreads of old ideas. I want to storm heaven, not curate a museum.

But Royce's method is fresh, exciting, and workable. It is disarmingly—almost inconceivably—simple, and its results are remarkable. To offer just one personal example: I was nearing an article deadline for a large national magazine. I had not begun my piece and didn't know how to do so. I was stymied. The clock was oppressively ticking. I used the scripting exercise, and in a day and a half I wrote a very solid article, which pleased my editors. This just doesn't happen. But there it was.

I've pondered this in connection with Roy Jarrett's work and now with Royce's: *Why* should something so simple work at all? Part of the answer, I believe, is that certain exercises get us selecting ideas and possibilities in our minds in a very concrete way. They break us out of habitual thought—and also out of inactive daydreams—and they enlist and focus our mental energies in a manner that we too rarely employ. Royce's method actually cuts *against* idle daydreaming or fantasy because of its fixed time frame: when you're thinking only twelve or so hours ahead, you are compelled to function within the framework of your current circumstances and possibilities. You cannot viably write something that is excessively fanciful, placing you on different continents, in different tax brackets, or with an adoring public at your feet. However the methodical nature of his exercise can serve to expand upon and build your potential circumstances. His longer ten-day exercise, which you will experience, helps gradually broaden your boundaries.

There is a brick-by-brick realism to Royce's approach . . . and something more. In my years as a seeker and writer within New Thought, I have come to feel that we do not manifest events. I believe, rather, that amid varying laws and forces under which we must live, we are able, through perspective, focus, mental pictures, and emotionalized thoughts, to *select* events from a nonlinear field of infinitude. I develop this theory in my book *The Miracle Club,* and I won't get into the weeds of it here. Suffice it to say, certain finely crafted and practicable exercises help us enter that field of selection. Some exercises work better than others, employing and engaging our psyches in the most productive ways. What you are about to experience is, in my view, one of those rare and remarkably effective methods that help galvanize your mental and emotional forces for maximum potency and results.

New Thought, as I've often said, is a philosophy of results—or it is nothing. To remain alive, vibrant, and generative, New Thought must identify methods that are persuasive, actionable, and doable within the framework of people's demanding lives. Royce's is one such method. And more. It is quite simply the freshest, most powerful, most persuasive technique that I've personally encountered since *It Works*. It is our generation's answer to the next generation, who will rightly ask, "What did you do to help move the ball down the field?" This is what we did. Read Royce's book and put it into action.

MITCH HOROWITZ is a PEN Award–winning historian, longtime publishing executive, and a leading New Thought commentator with bylines in *The New York Times, Time, Politico, Salon,* and *The Wall Street Journal* and media appearances on *Dateline NBC, CBS Sunday Morning, All Things Considered,* and *Coast to Coast AM.* He is the author of several books, including *Occult America, One Simple Idea,* and *The Miracle Club.* He lives in New York City.

Introduction

You Were Right

Great is the reward to those who help and give without thought of self, as it is impossible to be unselfish without gain.

R. H. J., *It Works*

LET'S NOT MINCE WORDS: you are holding in your hands the ingredients, recipe, and cookbook to change your life for the better, forever. Scripting is one of the most powerful tools any modern human can have in their arsenal. Whether you're a stay-at-home mom, CEO, student, or haven't decided yet what you want to be when you grow up, what you're about to learn to do will change your life. It actually scared me when, after years of trial and error, I finally figured out how to script the right way (there is a right way). It's easy, fun, and very simple.

I'm not going to lie to you either: scripting can be used for good or bad. It can be used as a major life tool to achieve goals, receive money, travel, find a mate, or get whatever else it is that you want. I hope that by the end of this book you will use this tool for good. But, ultimately, it's up to you and where your ethics and morals stand when it comes to what you choose to create in your reality. As you will soon realize, my good friend Mitch Horowitz scripted the book you now hold in your hands into existence (technically Mitch and I and YOU, dear reader, *all* scripted this book into reality—we will get to that a little later). All it takes is a pen and a cheap notebook or journal. Or your laptop. Or your phone. Like a match or a lighter, scripting is an inexpensive tool that has the potential to create massive change. You can light a candle or light a Burning Man–style effigy/bonfire with a match. The power is in how you *use* the tools (whatever they may be)—always.

Perhaps you have heard of scripting before. *Scripting* is about as vague a word to me as *cooking;* until I know what kind of cuisine is being cooked, how it is being cooked, and who is cooking it, the word means very little. When I first read about scripting (and we will dive into this more later in the book), it essentially meant that you talked out loud like a crazy person for ten or so minutes. The idea as it was most commonly taught was to pretend that you were talking (or writing) to an old friend as if some huge dream of yours had already come true. For example, the instructions on scripting I first read back in 2003 told me that since I would have to talk to myself, I needed to find a place where others wouldn't look at me like I was insane (like in my car), and pick a big desire on which to focus. Then I was instructed to start talking about how great it was now that I had my desire/dream come true. Basically, if you pretended that you already had your desire and talked about how great it was to have it, it would happen.

So let's say you wanted to be president of the United States. If you were to use scripting as it is most commonly taught, you would first go into your car or a quiet room in your house. Then you would pretend that you were on the phone with a friend and, with all the positive feelings and emotion inside of you, start "scripting" something out loud like this:

Wow! What an incredible inauguration! The whole day was a whirlwind and amazing. I loved the salad they served at the ball. There was this dressing that the White House chef made that was the most delicious vinaigrette I've ever tasted. I still can't believe I am waking up to go to work in the Oval Office every day. It is just incredible!

Other variations on the idea of scripting are just regurgitations of the above. They say that instead of talking out loud, write out a desire like it's already happened. They always tell you to really feel every single thing you are writing as if it's already happened. Savor every word, smell the smells, FEEL IT! Now, don't get me wrong, there is actually some good advice buried in there, and, believe it or not, there's some great groundwork in the original idea behind scripting. I guess it could be considered a sort of "out loud" (or written) visualization of your big dreams.

But, when it comes right down to it, like many visualization techniques, this method of scripting isn't very effective. It, like so many of the tools and exercises espoused by well-meaning self-help or New Thought teachers, puts many people in an even worse state of mind than they were before, or it leaves them extremely frustrated. The problem is that, as with many methods taught to help us have the life of our dreams, creating a "new life script" is really *a lot* to ask a person staring down the reality of desires not already in front of them. It just feels weird to be sitting in your used car outside of the apartment you share with five people, "talking" on the phone about the private jet you just bought. Or it's unrealistic to be in the house you share with your hubby and two toddlers writing about how wonderful your new gig as a back-up dancer for Beyoncé has been.

For me the most frustrating part is that you actually *can* have those things; you really *can* be anything you want and have anything you want even if it seems impossible. The most successful people know this is true (though many may keep quiet about it, often unintentionally or naturally, so they won't attribute it to any special power or "law"). One of the reasons I wrote this book is that I am living proof you can make your dreams come true with some really awesome methods or hacks like scripting. Also I'm sick of people who teach this stuff not talking about the *real* methods that work.

Despite the many issues with creating a new life script that I encountered when I first tried it, I continued to do it because for every hundred times scripting didn't work, there was one or two times when it worked in ways that baffled me. So I knew *there was something there that worked,* but there was a problem with the method that I couldn't quite place. I wasn't even looking for a problem, but I kept observing that the success rate of scripting (not only for me but also for other friends who were trying this generally accepted and understood way to script) was, well, pretty dismal.

It worked about 5 percent of the time for me (okay, maybe 10 percent of the time, if I'm being generous). But that small percentage of the time that it worked was enough for me to keep trying to figure out if there was a way to make it work 100 percent of the time. I *knew* there was something to scripting, and no matter how much I tried to ignore it, the *"There is something here, Royce!"* repeating over and over in my mind wouldn't shut up.

Here's the other problem I found over my life as a student of this stuff: a lot of people who teach self-help, New Thought, or spiritual techniques often don't have all of the information, lie, leave out some hugely important instructions, oversimplify, play down to their base audience, try to gain too big an audience, or just try so damn hard to reinvent that poor original stone wheel of New Thought and positive thinking that it basically just becomes a pile of dust. The other thing is that many teachers are scared to talk about how all this creating your life the way you want it to be *really* works . . . if they even know how it all really works. Or, if they do consider talking about all of it, they are ridiculed, or afraid of being ridiculed.

Look, I'm not dissing New Thought teachers. Anyone brave enough to go into the public sphere and teach this stuff has my respect. Some teachers don't even know they are lying or withholding some key steps to certain methods. Why? *Because whatever they are teaching has been repeated from the original source in SO MANY BOOKS over the past hundred years or so that the new teachers don't even know they are lying by omission.* This is because, at some point, key steps were left out, and then many, many, many authors and well-meaning teachers repeated the fill-in-the-blank method (or tool) with the missing steps. There is no secret; there is just a pile of old discoveries and ideas being repackaged as "new" or "hidden" with missing steps. I've found that a lot of people are afraid to get down in the trenches, get their hands dirty, and test these methods. Well, that isn't how I operate.

It took me almost four years from the day I first read about scripting back in 2003 to figure out the key to it. That was with working at it almost daily for those four years, throwing away what didn't work, keeping what did, dismantling the construct, and rebuilding it from the ground up until I figured out what did work: building an entirely new wheel instead of trying to reinvent the old one. I was (and am) extremely lucky because I was raised in a family that taught me about positive thinking, New Thought, and self-help principles from a very young age. My unique scripting method isn't the only tool I have in my toolbox, but it is as important to creating whatever I want in my life as solid earth is to building a home.

I was nineteen years old when I landed on the winning recipe, as it were, to scripting. Since I was raised with my mom and grandma teaching me this stuff and already had a good handle on much of it, it was always easy to learn or create a new way of utilizing a New Thought technique . . . and I was usually able to do so very quickly. So, for me, the fact that it took four solid years for me to figure out scripting was unusual. The payoff, however, was (and still continues to be) incredibly worth it. Here's the good news about my method:

- It doesn't require you to talk to yourself out loud like a crazy person or write long-winded stories about things that seem impossible to you.
- It is extremely flexible and easy to learn.
- It works. Fast.

Look, to be totally honest, I originally figured out this scripting method for purely selfish reasons. I wanted, really badly, to book a certain acting job on a certain TV show. I happened to land on the right scripting method a few weeks before the role was set to be cast, and my scripting method worked. It worked for a lot of stuff. It works really, really well for many things.

Am I a psychopath who will tell you that scripting will cure your disease and tell you not to go to your doctor? No. *Go to the doctor.* Am I insane and going to tell you that because people weren't scripting or using positive thinking they died in some horrible catastrophe or disaster? No. All of that kind of talk is crap, and I hate when "teachers" blame victims.

Have I tripped, screwed up at times, and stopped my unique scripting practice at any point in my life since I was nineteen? YES. Have I since realized that it is a foundational tool and that it is stupid for me to stop doing it for a long period of time? Yup. Have I figured out that there is A LOT of new and even more exciting stuff when it comes to creating and manifesting your dreams besides scripting? YES. But my friend Mitch, who wrote the foreword, was right when he said that I needed to write a book about scripting.

For us to venture into the future of New Thought, manifesting, and creating the life of our dreams, we need a foundation that is solid. I am excited to talk to you about scripting, and that will be the bulk of this book. This is because it works, and it is my intention that you benefit greatly from knowing how to do it and put it into action. But we will also talk about the future and how groundbreaking new technology and science (other than the exhaustively and often incorrectly used quantum physics) point to incredible new ways to create our reality—and why they might actually work.

Don't let the word *manifest* scare you off. Have you ever shopped online? If so, you've manifested. Have you ever shopped on Amazon using their Prime service? Can you imagine what the original teachers of New Thought, positive thinking, and manifesting from a hundred, fifty, or even fifteen years ago would think about our world today if you told them that you can now think about a coffee mug, pull up a photo of that mug on a magic screen (your tablet or computer), tap your finger on that magic screen, and then have that exact coffee mug appear on your front doorstep two hours later? They would lose their minds with excitement!

We are living in a world where instant manifestation is getting closer and closer to being in, if not already a part of, our reality. Scripting, and all we are about to talk about, is really as easy as ordering that coffee mug off Amazon. Or downloading a song. Or reading a book.

One

Excuse Me,
Your Life Is Waiting

Everyone has been remarkably influenced by a book, or books. In my case it was a book on cartoon animation. I discovered it in the Kansas City Library at the time I was preparing to make motion-picture animation my life's work. Finding that book was one of the most important and useful events in my life. It happened at just the right time. The right time for reading a story or an article or a book is important.

WALT DISNEY

I CAN STILL REMEMBER THE CAR RIDE where my mom handed me the book that changed the course of my life forever. From guest starring with Selena Gomez on an Emmy award–winning sitcom to directing documentaries to meeting the person I consider my soul mate, it still creeps me out (in a good way) that so much of what happened next and continues to happen in my life I can attribute to that one, very short moment in time when my mom reached from her position in the front passenger seat of my dad's truck to the backseat where I was sitting and handed me a book she had been reading but not enjoying very much.

It was the summer of 2003, and I was fifteen years old. My mom, dad, sister, and I were driving from our house in Marlton, New Jersey, to Virginia's Eastern Shore. I can still remember the air that day and how it changed as we drove south. When we left our house that morning, the air carried a heat that reminded me of a steam room, where it feels like you could fill an empty cup with water just by holding it up in the saturated air for long enough. As we drove farther, it was still warm, but the air shifted to a crisper, slightly cooler temperature. We thought it might rain that day but were surprised by how bright and sunny the whole drive was. There wasn't one single cloud in the sky. It was so computer-simulated perfect that it almost didn't look real.

This drive was a ritual for my small family. It was one of a few yearly sojourns that we took during those sticky summer months to what is affectionately called the "Delmarva Peninsula," a small sliver of land that starts in Delaware (*Del*), follows into Maryland (*mar*), and finishes in Virginia (*va*). It is separated from the mainland of the United States by the vast, salty Chesapeake Bay.

Of the many cities and small towns that dot Delmarva, our family had a special connection with two small barrier islands that lay just off the Atlantic coast. Right where the border of Maryland meets Virginia are Assateague and Chincoteague Islands. Assateague is a rugged national park where wild horses run free (yes, for real!) and no man lives. It is connected by a small bridge to Chincoteague Island, a small Virginia town that has somehow managed to simultaneously keep up with modern advancements and retain a sense of early 1900s small-town American charm. People who want to spend a few days visiting the unspoiled Assateague Island choose to stay in one of the many small hotels and bed and breakfasts on Chincoteague.

My mom found out that she was pregnant with me when she was visiting these islands in the summer of 1987. She had suffered a miscarriage the summer before and wasn't sure if she would be able to get pregnant again. One of the unique things about the beach on Assateague Island is that you are allowed to drive your truck out onto the sand that runs between the ocean and the bay. This allows for some very cool beach experiences. There are not many other people around like you would normally expect from a typical summer beach retreat. Sometimes there are no people at all.

My mom was standing on the beach watching my dad surf-fishing and admiring the sun as it began its increasingly rapid descent below the horizon. It would be a full moon that night, and just as it began to get dark, with the first stars shimmering in the sky, she saw what she describes as a backward-falling star.

"What the hell is a backward-falling star?" I can remember asking her the first time she told me the story of the night she knew she was pregnant with me.

"It was exactly what it sounds like," she answered. "Instead of the star falling from the sky and dissipating as it got close to land (or in this case, the vast Atlantic ocean), it did the opposite. The star—or whatever it was—came bursting out of the ocean and flew upward in an arc until it dissipated in the sky."

(STOP. *Before you close this book, my mom doesn't believe in aliens and that is not where this is going, so don't jump to conclusions.* This is important backstory. If you want to know how to change or enhance your life, you've come to the right place. Just hang in there and agree to follow along with me so I can get you in Life-Transforming Mode as quickly as possible!) Now, moving on . . .

My mom yelled to my dad to see if he had seen the "falling star" too. He couldn't hear her over the sound of the crashing waves, so he walked out of the few feet of water he was standing in and went up onto the dry sand to where she was waving her arms. She told him what she had just seen. As she was talking to my dad, she glanced over to the spot in the ocean right where my dad had just been standing moments before and almost fell over from what she spotted.

As the sun was taking its final bow below the horizon, she could easily see the reflection of a giant shark fin and, about seven feet behind it, a smaller tail fin. Had she not called my dad over in that exact moment, he likely would have been Jaws's appetizer for the night (if not his whole dinner!). For some reason, immediately after both of those moments passed, my mom had this overwhelming sense that she was pregnant. When they arrived home from their trip a few days later, her doctor confirmed that she was indeed pregnant with me—and only about three to four weeks pregnant at that.

Many people will make different assumptions about this story— the star, the shark, and how those two things combined equated to my mom knowing that she was pregnant with no physical feelings or signs. But for our family, it was just the first of many serendipitous events that seemed to always surround our trips to these two special islands over the years.

As we drove closer to the island on that fateful day in 2003, my mind became unusually consumed with negative thoughts. I was dealing with typical just-turned-fifteen-years-old problems as I had just had a very rare (for us, as we never fought) argument with my best friend the night before we left for vacation. It was an incredibly awful fight—more akin to an explosion. It was one of those fights that sometimes leads people to stop being friends completely.

As we drove toward the islands, I was angry that I had no way of fixing the situation. This was when texting cost ten cents or more per text *and* before the current age where ten new ways to communicate with people are invented every day. My point is: I couldn't fix this situation easily until we got home from our family trip, and it was eating me up inside. I was also stuck in the truck with my family.

I hated fighting with my best friend, and I had *never* won the few arguments we had in the past. I remember thinking about it over and over again because although drama is typical of high schoolers, my friends and I rarely experienced it among ourselves. I was also still in the closet, knew it, and was feeling anxious overall (just a few months later I would come out to my parents and friends under really good circumstances). Needless to say, there was a lot going on inside of me at that particular moment.

I tried to calm myself down. I reached for my trusted portable CD player and binder of CDs, trying to find the right music that might put me in a better mood. Just as I settled into the first sixty seconds of Madonna's song "Erotica," the music stopped. The AA batteries in the CD player had died, and I hadn't brought any extras with me like I normally would have. My mood got worse, and my mom noticed.

GREAT MOM . . . BAD BOOK?

My mom and I have always been very, very connected. She often knew something was wrong before I did (she still does). She knew I needed something to make me feel better. Back then, she found herself enrolled in a mail-order book club that would send her books every month. The funny thing is, to this day, she swears that she never enrolled in this book club. One day the books just started coming to our house. She liked the books, so she paid for them and stayed in the club.

One of the books she had received in the mail a week before our trip was from a little-known author named Lynn Grabhorn. The book was titled *Excuse Me, Your Life Is Waiting*. This was one of the first modern books that dealt with the Law of Attraction, having originally been published in 1999, seven years before *The Secret* took the Law mainstream for a new generation. My mom wasn't enjoying the book, as she was familiar with the ideas it presented due to her own upbringing in the teachings of positive thinking and New Thought. But she thought it might get my mind off things, so she suggested that I read it.

Within ten minutes of reading, I asked if anyone in the car had a highlighter. My dad, who always managed to carry a bizarre collection of pens, pencils, and writing utensils in his truck, handed me a bright yellow highlighter. I was fascinated by the book, entranced by its contents. Here was a person who was writing about something I always wanted to know: How *exactly* do you create in your life the things, people, and circumstances that you want . . . on command?

I had been introduced to the concept of creating your life the way that you wanted it to be, yet most books focused on theory and not implementation or action. Lynn Grabhorn explained both so effortlessly, and with such ease, it was like I had found home inside a book. I stopped highlighting by page 100, because almost every page was bright yellow from my marks.

The best part? The author wasn't just talking about positive think-ing or visualization or any of the "self-help-lite" things that most books covering these topics discussed. To be clear, these things are great and helpful and can be extraordinarily effective . . . *if* you know what needs to come first: the understanding that we create by feeling and emotions (a combination of our emotions and the vibrations that we emit from having them), *which are generated from thought and circumstance, not by thought alone.* She also made clear what Mitch Horowitz writes about in many of his books: *you must select a chief, ultimate goal and be all in with that goal.*

Though I was young, I knew in my gut that this was right. At the very least, it *felt* right. Which is more than I could say about any of the other books on the subject I had read up until that point. I devoured the book. I read its 305 pages three times over the course of my family vacation. But more importantly at the time? I also finally had a solution to my (then) most pressing fifteen-year-old crisis: a possible way to fix this ugly fight with my best friend.

GOOD VIBRATIONS

I have noticed that even people who claim everything is predetermined and that we can do nothing to change it look before they cross the road.

Stephen Hawking, *Black Holes and Baby Universes and Other Essays*

I felt empowered and armed with a secret weapon. Like I had overheard a giant secret or gotten the answers to a test ahead of time. I knew, somehow, someway, this book would be a key to helping me. Boy, was I right. But, boy, did I not fully comprehend how much the trajectory of my life changed in that moment my mom handed me the book. The book explained how it was not only positive thoughts but also the vibrations they emitted that caused our outside reality. Send out good vibrations, receive good things into our lives. Send out bad vibrations, guess what comes back? I was armed with a tool. Something to try. *Something new and different.*

I'm going to get this out of the way right now for my fellow skeptics and researchers: I am a researcher at heart. I am not a scientist, but science is my passion. One of my life intentions is to show the ever-present, though often very overlooked connection between all of this "woo-woo" stuff and science. It exists, but there are a few problems.

One major problem can be explained with the following analogy: A gardener who finds a seed, plants it in her garden, and grows a cucumber bush may end up writing many books about her own personal experiences working outside, planting in the dirt, growing the best cucumbers, and so on. This person is almost certainly not the same person who finds a seed, takes it to a lab, puts it under a microscope, and writes books about the chemical components and biological makeup of the cucumber seed.

These two individuals may write many books, but rarely would a situation arise where it would be crucial for them to read each other's books. In their minds, their areas of knowledge are set. The fans and readers of the scientist's books may point to the woman in her garden, who speaks of her time in the dirt, and laugh at her because they prefer the book by the person who has studied every cell of the cucumber seed.

In the end, which author's book would you pick up if you wanted to know how to grow cucumbers in your garden? The gardener may spend years finding what some would call woo-woo techniques that seem to increase her chances of having the best cucumbers. Maybe she plays music for her plants. Maybe she talks to them in the quiet mornings. Yet the scientist may laugh at the gardener, because the scientist's thirty-day controlled cucumber-growing experiment gave no hint that any of the off-the-wall, "unscientific" statements made by the gardener, who spent years in the dirt with her cucumbers, were true or even mattered.

Unfortunately this chasm between science and New Thought, positive thinking, vibrations, and all the things many people call "weird" or "woo-woo" is even greater when it comes to the topics

covered in this book. Mitch Horowitz explains the issue in his book
The Miracle Club:

> Many of the same journalists, social critics, and intellectuals who
> run down positive thinking, New Age, and self-help are all too
> eager to cite cognitive studies as proof of a favored idea because such
> reports seem to possess the sheen of peer-reviewed, clinically based
> sturdiness. A case in point arrived in 2015 with an article in the
> online opinion journal Aeon, in which journalist Elizabeth Svoboda
> sized up the self-help field. In her "Saved by the Book," Svoboda con-
> cluded that some cognitively based self-help books are effective—
> and well worth defending—while New Age and positive-thinking
> books are the product of "woo-peddlers" who cheapen the field.
>
> Svoboda's piece demonstrated two assumptions that make it dif-
> ficult to gainfully discuss self-help therapeutics in much of today's
> media. First, the author groups together two different kinds of
> books: metaphysical works, such as the perennial critic's punching
> bag *The Secret,* and books based on clinical study, such as *Feeling
> Good* by David D. Burns, M.D. Although their authors share some
> concerns, such books have little in common: one represents theology
> and the other cognitive therapy.[1]

Horowitz's point is blunt: many who decry books like the one you
now hold in your hands are often upset about a "lack of science." But
there is a place for science and a place for belief systems. The points at
which they intersect are increasing, as we will explore in this book.

I wasn't aware of any of these debates when I first read *Excuse Me,
Your Life Is Waiting.* Grabhorn told me that vibrations created my reality. Here's the thing: when it comes to vibrations—specifically the idea
that the body, emotions, and feelings create certain vibrations that act
like magnets to bring to us people, events, and circumstances that cor-
respond with said vibrational frequencies—the science is, well, shaky at
best and not there at worst.

But the reason the science is not there is because of a *massive* lack of *proper* studies. Yet there is incredible new science on how we *do* create our realities, and it will blow your mind. Like I said, I'm a total science and research geek. What I've discovered in just the past two years is that everyone—believers and nonbelievers alike—has been looking for the wrong science. They've been googling the wrong things. We all have.

When it comes to human vibrations, we have two groups of people, both looking for the wrong thing. On one side of the argument, we have a group of believers in the frequency-circumstance connection theory. Their point is that just because there haven't been studies (or, more properly, enough studies) to prove frequencies from emotions and feelings correlate to real-life circumstances doesn't mean the phenomenon isn't real. The other side says that there isn't even enough anecdotal evidence to warrant said studies in the first place.

So you won't have to read page after page of both sides of this argument, let's stop here. (*Spoiler alert*: there is a real, actual scientific field of study that proves that emotions, feelings, and thoughts create our reality, but it has nothing to do with frequencies or even quantum mechanics. It's something much easier to understand, and there are studies, and books, and research papers to prove it!)

LOBSTER IN A DRESS SHOP

The problem is that both critics and believers alike have been looking in the wrong place for a long time. Like my grandma always told me: you're never going to be able to buy a lobster in a dress shop. But just because you won't find a single lobster at any dress shop in the world doesn't mean that lobsters don't exist; it simply means that you're looking for them in the wrong store.

You have to decide right now if you believe in magic and miracles or not. If you don't want to make that decision yet, decide that you will have an open mind as you read forward. I understand that if your life has been shitty as of late (or for years or decades on end), you may not believe in much of anything right now, let alone magic. Miracles may seem dim or dumb or even delusional to entertain at this point.

I get it. Believe it or not, I've been there. We all have. The thing is, you may only *think* that you don't believe in magic or miracles anymore. And maybe you truly don't, but I'd lay wager that you could just be experiencing a major case of hopelessness. *And that's okay.*

On the other hand, you may be living an excellent, exquisite life and be ready to expand the amazingness. You have hope and are excited about the future. I know I am. Look, if we are going to get anything out of life, we need some hope. That is why I don't make any promises in this book that I can't keep. It really is all about you and how and if you apply this relatively easy method of scripting to your life. I love science way more than most people, and that has served me well throughout my life. I lean toward skeptical, if I'm being honest. So I promise that you are going to learn about some incredible science that gives bones to the muscle and tissue of this book. Science is a friend of the "creating your own reality" community. Contrary to what many espouse, *science is not the enemy of spirit.*

I didn't know anything about this science versus spirit debate when my mom gave me the book that changed my life forever, and I'm happy about that. I studied the book up and down during my entire vacation on the islands. I don't even remember the beach from that trip! I was enthralled with what I read and beyond eager to test out the methods Grabhorn suggested. She said they would put me in charge of my circumstances, so I wouldn't be a victim any longer, and that sounded great to me! Twenty years later, her book still remains solid and ahead of its time. It accomplishes so much, and, in my opinion, it is one of the most underrated contributions to the library of New Thought books in the world.

Two

Scary, Terrifying Miracles

Knowledge is like underwear. It is useful to have it, but not necessary to show it off.

ATTRIBUTED TO BILL MURRAY

AT ITS CORE, *Excuse Me, Your Life Is Waiting* covered what I now refer to as the basics of manifesting. Grabhorn added her own unique ideas and changes to Jerry and Esther Hicks's teachings of Abraham. (If you haven't heard of Abraham-Hicks, their teachings are the foundations for almost all of the modern information on creating your own reality; I highly recommend taking a look at their books and their Abraham-Hicks website.)

Grabhorn had some really interesting exercises in the book, one of which was scripting, and I tried everything she suggested. Before I even got home from my vacation (without even knowing 100 percent exactly what I was doing), I started "pushing out" the best feelings I could muster. I didn't want to be in this fight with my best friend any longer.

Grabhorn boiled down the process of how to get what you want into four basic steps:

1. Know what you don't want.
2. Find out what you do want.
3. Get into the feeling place of having the want(s).

4. Allow the thing you want to come into your life (a.k.a. be open to receiving, or chill out and let what you've asked for arrive).

I started to think about the best friend with whom I was fighting and tried to feel (and think) all the positive things I could about her. I knew what I didn't want: to be in this fight. I knew what I did want: relief, happiness, and joy with my best friend. So, according to the book, I had to "get into the feeling place" of what I wanted, conditions be damned.

This made things easy. I could use all of the good times I had over the years with my friend as a back door into feeling good. By conjuring up real memories from real experiences, I could *re-feel* how wonderful the friendship was. Doing this really worked, and it felt really, really good.

One thing that I liked, even at such a young age, was that the author didn't suggest that I *always* had to pretend. According to her book, if I was focusing on the fight with my best friend being over and behind us, my focus was squarely on where I didn't want my focus to be: the fight. But she also understood that we are human, and pretending isn't always easy when it comes to tough situations.

It's the same principle you hear over and over again when it comes to vibrations, positive thinking, New Thought principles, and the Law of Attraction: the Universe (or God, or whatever term you want to use) doesn't hear "I don't want to be sick." According to this way of thinking, the Universe only hears the word *sick*. This is, as Grabhorn explained, a result of our emotionally charged vibrations attached to the "don't want."

In other words, we may think we are telling the Universe we want to be healthy by saying, "I don't want to be *sick*," but look at what word we are focusing on: *sick*. By the same token, if we are saying, "I want to be *healthy*," we are pointing out that we are *not healthy*, because it is something we want and therefore do not currently have. I know you probably feel like your head is spinning off. Don't worry, I have spent my life figuring out the tricks and hacks to get around all of this nonsense doublespeak.

So, to reiterate using my example: even though I might have thought I was stating a "want" by saying, "I don't want to be in this fight with my best friend," I was actually still telling the universe a "don't want" because I was emphasizing the word *fight*: "fight, fight with my best friend, fight—more fight, please." In *Excuse Me, Your Life Is Waiting*, Grabhorn explained that this is because our thoughts create our emotions, and our emotions create our feelings, which in turn create highly charged positive or negative vibrations. These vibrations go out into the Universe and come back to us like a boomerang. According to Grabhorn, we can only pull things into our experience that are vibrating at the same frequency as the thoughts and emotions we are sending out. Like attracts like. Get it? This made so much sense to fifteen-year-old me, and I was hooked. I really was hating this stupid fight with my friend, and I knew I had been focusing on it way too much. This book felt like the answer to all my prayers.

In the book, Grabhorn also references a study[1] in which scientists wanted to see if they could photograph vibrations of thought in an attempt to prove thoughts were things. The scientists not only succeeded in doing so (through steel walls, no less), but they also found that the more emotionally charged a thought was, the clearer the picture came out. Grabhorn states:

> What [the scientists] missed, though, is that because the vibrational waves (emotions) we send out are magnetically charged, we are literally walking magnets, constantly pulling back into our world anything that just happens to be playing on the same frequency or wavelength.
>
> For instance, when we're feeling up, filled with joy and gratitude, our emotions are sending out high-frequency vibrations that will magnetize only good stuff back to us, meaning anything with the same high vibratory frequency that matches what we're sending out. Like attracts like.
>
> On the other hand, when we're experiencing anything that joy isn't, such as fear, worry, guilt, or even mild concern, those emotions

are sending out low-frequency vibrations. Since low frequencies are every bit as magnetic as high frequencies, they're going to attract only cruddy stuff back to us, meaning anything of that same low frequency that will cause us to feel (and vibrate) as lousy as what we're sending out. Cruddy out, cruddy back; it's always a vibrational match.[2]

I realized I had been putting out hours and hours of negative vibrations into the world because of this fight with my best friend. Grabhorn scared me when she said that when we were feeling bad, we weren't only attracting back to us the thing we were feeling bad about. *We were also pulling in anything on the same matching frequency as the yucky thing.* Your negative vibrations about a flat tire, she explained, were causing an electromagnetic signal that pulled other crappy stuff into your life.

That flat tire vibration, if felt long enough, would be sent out there into the world where billions of other people were sending their vibrations—low and high. Whatever yours matched up with would come back to you. That flat tire boomerang of negative frequency might end up "matching" you with also getting an unexpected bill, having a fight with your employer, and food poisoning.

No thanks. I was a geeky kid in elementary school, and I worked hard to get a group of friends in high school that not only accepted me for who I was, but who were also liked by other kids who might have otherwise bullied me, so I wasn't a punching bag. I didn't want this one fight with my best friend vibrationally attracting a domino effect of negativity into my life. So I searched for exercises in her book that I could do, sort of as a test, to see if what she was writing about really worked. I landed on scripting.

The minute we got home from our island vacation, I ran up to my bathroom, turned on the shower (so no one would hear me), and did as Grabhorn suggested: I started talking, out loud, as if I was talking to my best friend. I pretended it was a few weeks into the future and didn't even bring up the fight in our "conversation." I felt this good sensation in my stomach that I found I could almost push into an even better feeling. I can, to this day, only liken it to butterflies (but the good kind) that we feel in our stomach when we're excited, but these butterflies were ones I could control and intensify at will. Once I felt this stirring of positive butterflies in my stomach, I could physically push it outward and make it grow.

I talked for more than fifteen minutes about how great the past few weeks had been (pretending it was now three weeks in the future). I reminisced about some made up sleepover where we ordered ten pizzas (something we would never do because there were only a few of us in our core group of friends, and most of us had stingy parents). I talked and talked, scripting out loud as the book instructed. I talked to her about plans to go to a different beach than we normally did, and how maybe we would see that cute guy she met earlier in the summer. I could actually feel my brain buzzing and was almost light-headed. It felt, genuinely, really good. After I "hung up" our conversation, I realized that I should probably actually take a shower (since the water was on anyway).

Within sixty seconds of being in the shower, my flip phone rang (remember, this was 2003 . . .). It was my best friend, who hadn't tried to call me for days. I jumped out of the shower, naked and soaking wet, and reached to pick up the phone. Trembling with a mixture of fear and excitement I thought to myself, "Is this really happening? Does it really work this fast?"

In those last few seconds before I answered, I was still feeling the wonderful "after buzz" of my out-loud scripting. However, since this whole "creating my world the way I want it" stuff was brand new, I was fully expecting her to yell at me and for me to yell back. The fight was very raw, and we had left it on a firm "to be continued" note when I departed for the islands with my family.

"Hello . . ." I said hesitantly into the phone.

"Hey! Do you wanna go down to the shore tonight and stay at my grandparents' beach house for a few days?" she asked, bubbly, cheerful, and without a hint of irony or anger.

"I . . . Yes!" I answered. "That sounds fun. I'd love to . . ." I stopped talking midsentence and looked into the bathroom mirror to make sure I was awake and not dreaming. I was in shock and relieved but also supremely confused. My brain was not computing what was happening. I am not someone who overreacts or exaggerates, so let me be clear: when we got into this fight before my vacation, there was a *strong* possibility that our friendship would be over for good because of how bad it had been. My usually bubbly, talkative side shut down completely at her sudden about-face.

"Are you okay?" She asked.

"Yeah . . . I am *now*. I just . . . I figured after the . . ."

She interrupted me before I could even finish my sentence: "You mean that argument we had? I'm over it, and I'm sorry. I should have called and apologized earlier, but you were gone and I didn't want to ruin your vacation. I'm over it; let's move on. I wasn't being fair. I miss you! Let's go to the beach tonight."

I was flabbergasted. This was not a person who apologized (to be fair, neither was I at the time). She was not someone to let *anything* go, let alone a potentially friendship-altering fight. Then she said something that made me almost fall on the wet floor.

"Oh! By the way, we are thinking about going to the Ocean City boardwalk instead of Ventnor. I'm hoping . . ."

"You might . . . see . . . that cute guy we met earlier this summer. . . ?" I stammered, barely getting it out.

My mind was exploding. See, of the many traits my best friend and I had in common, one big one was that, in addition to both of us being extremely recalcitrant, we never (ever!) changed the beach or boardwalk we went to—for years our summer adventures were the same. We always stayed in Margate City (a beautiful beach town at the Jersey Shore where her family had a huge beach house), and we *always* went to the boardwalk in Ventnor. I am not even sure why I added the idea of us going to a different beach into my scripting conversation. If anything, it was to test the method, and, right then, the method felt like it was testing *my* limits of what was possible.

She laughed. "Yes! You sound so weird right now. I heard the hot guy likes to hang out at the Ocean City boardwalk, so I figured it's worth a shot. Get ready. My dad will pick us up and take us down around 4:00."

We hung up and I sat down on my bathroom floor, contemplating the seeming impossibility of what had just happened. *Everything* about the conversation in real life I just had not only *correlated* with the story I had told in my out-loud pretend scripting conversation, but, even better, the emotions of happiness and relief where now *genuinely* buzzing all over me. I was in shock. IT WORKED!

My best friend, the most stubborn human being I knew on Earth (other than myself) was just letting the fight of a lifetime go? We were going to a different boardwalk? To hopefully run into the cute guy she had met earlier that summer? JUST LIKE I HAD SCRIPTED OUT LOUD NOT EVEN FIVE MINUTES EARLIER?!

I finished my shower and got ready to go down to the shore. I was, I must admit, in a bit of a zombielike state the first hour. I was thrilled that the fight was over but also floored at how easily scripting, vibrations, and this so-called Law of Attraction seemed to work. At the boardwalk we ran into the guy my best friend had been pining over, and he and his friends joined us. Later that night we ended up meeting a few more friends, and we all went back to my best friend's grandparents' beach house where we always slept.

When we got to the house around 8:00 p.m., my best friend's dad said he had a surprise for us. Earlier he had gone to get a couple of pizzas, but the pizza joint was having some crazy special, and there on the kitchen counter were not the usual two boxes of pizza; instead there were *ten boxes of pizza* waiting for us to enjoy. I lost my appetite.

I looked around, wondering how this was happening. It may seem like such little things in retrospect, but to me, it was proof that this book held some sort of magical key to life. As happy as I was to be with my best friend and all of our other friends at the beach house enjoying pizza, all I wanted to do was go home and reread the book again. I wanted to try other things the book recommended. I was elated.

I was also terrified. If it was really this easy to change things around me, I reasoned, then I couldn't be the only one who knew about this "magical" information. I started overthinking and, in my then-typical fashion, freaked out. Was everyone doing this? Could everyone do this?

THE UNIVERSE MUGGED ME

My ability to turn good news into anxiety is rivaled only by my ability to turn anxiety into chin acne.

Tina Fey, *Bossypants*

I acted weirdly for the rest of the weekend at the beach. At least that is what all of my friends kept saying (and I knew why; I just didn't tell them). I hadn't brought the book with me to the beach, but I had studied it so much on my vacation the previous weekend that I knew enough to keep playing with the ideas it presented. I tried to remain in as good of a feeling place as possible. If someone said something weird, or something I didn't like happened, I would run up to the bathroom of the beach house and start thinking about how I wanted the situation to shift or change. I would figure out the feeling I wanted to get from changing the situation, and then I would think of something to trigger the emotion that got me into that new, wanted feeling place. For the most part, it worked.

When I finally got home from the shore with my friends, I felt like a god. Only about a week and a half had passed between the day my mom first handed me the book and the day I got home from the beach with my friends. I finally went to talk to my mom about everything. When she had first handed me *Excuse Me, Your Life Is Waiting,* she hadn't said much. When, on the family vacation, she noticed I couldn't put the book down, she mentioned that she was happily surprised, as she really didn't enjoy reading it that much. I remembered this as I sat down at the kitchen table to talk with her. I couldn't understand why she didn't like a book that taught people how to create whatever they wanted in their lives.

My family was full of very unique and spiritual people who believed in things that most would consider outside of the norm. My mom and grandmother started teaching me concepts related to creating your own reality when I was very, very young. When most of my friends were going to Hebrew school and Sunday school, they were teaching me how to meditate and write down affirmations. So, while the concept of creating my own reality was not *new* to me, this "creating on demand" that the book taught me was completely foreign . . . and awesome! I was used to things taking time, which was, up until that moment, very okay with me. In fact I had already used tools like affirmations and meditation to create some incredible things in my life by age fifteen.

While I believed we could do many things to create in our lives, my family's methods used a lot of steps, and things took time to come to fruition, if they did at all. The simplicity of what Grabhorn taught in her book was also one of the things that made this all so shocking to me. If it was as easy as talking out loud with scripting and getting into the right emotional feeling place, my fifteen-year-old self was convinced that I would be a billionaire within a few weeks.

My mom was very supportive of my enthusiasm for the book. She admitted that she had only been a few chapters in when she handed it to me. I told her everything that had happened with using not only scripting but also with pushing out good feelings (vibrations). She told me it sounded great and to keep studying it and applying it to see what happened. I was so thrilled with the book that I was planning on using this new "magic power" no matter what my mother said, but it was nice that she was encouraging me to dive right in to the work.

You have to keep in mind that this was the year 2003, and, while the internet existed, it was *not* what it is today—at all. Even the *idea* of using it to search for anything and everything—whether that was to find others who studied this topic or the source information from Abraham-Hicks the author briefly (and I do mean briefly) mentioned in the book—was just not a thing in the year 2003. YouTube, social media, and much of what they consider to be our current Internet 2.0 didn't exist at all, and this was a few years before *The Secret* took some of the ideas Grabhorn presented in her book into the mainstream.

So I had this one book to go off of, and I was excited to do everything it told me to do. I set up a game plan of sorts for the next few years, which consisted of a simple list of my desires:

1. I want to have a large part in the school play and musical.
2. I want a boyfriend.
3. I want to graduate early.
4. I want to transition from acting in professional theater to acting in TV and film.
5. I want to move to Los Angeles to pursue my career.

Now, remember that at that time I was fifteen; it was pretty unheard of for a freshman-about-to-be-sophomore to get a lead role, and I was not next in line to be more than chorus in the school play and musical; I was in the closet, and I only knew of one person who was out of the closet at my high school of more than a thousand people; I had no path to graduating early and no idea how this was going to happen; I had never taken a class on acting on film—only theater; and I lived three thousand miles from Los Angeles. But none of these seemed like obstacles to me, because I now knew there was a way to get whatever it was in life I wanted. It all seemed so easy!

I spent a few weeks honing my manifesting skills. I worked on creating lists of *why* I wanted what I wanted. I kept scripting out loud and scripting in my notebooks, pretending as if I were in some nebulous future where everything I wanted had already come true. I kept pushing out really good vibrations and emotions. I was feeling really good overall. I felt like I knew the secret to creating miracles.

Then I told my friends about the book.

To say they called me stupid would be a lie. They weren't mean friends who made me feel like an idiot or called me names. But . . . they definitely made me want to throw *Excuse Me, Your Life Is Waiting* into a dumpster with some gasoline and a lit match. I tried not to let it get to me, but, it was clear: everyone thought this stuff was stupid. I didn't change anything, they told me. They laughed at the idea that someone could change their reality. I was wasting my time, they said. Even some of my nonspiritual family members laughed when I told them about what I had been up to and how well it seemed to be working.

Look, the year was 2003, and I didn't know then what I know now. Oddly, I did get everything I had on my Want List above (more on that later), but I figured I got these things by using the more traditional methods my mom had taught me (that I, wisely, never told my friends or extended family about) combined with some plain old hard work. I wish I could tell you that I secretly kept working on the methods from the book, but I did not. I put the book away and told myself I was done with it.

Then I got mugged.

Three

Step One:
Write Your Daily Want List

There's nowhere you can be that isn't where you're meant to be.

THE BEATLES,
"ALL YOU NEED IS LOVE"

IT TOOK GETTING MUGGED and almost stabbed to death before I finally got the Universe's/God's/fill-in-the-blank's hint that I really needed to pay attention to the teachings of *Excuse Me, Your Life Is Waiting*. That book had the seed, and, as it would turn out, I had the soil, sun, and water to make a small idea grow into something that would transform my life (and now *your* life) forever.

I put the book down for eighteen months after I was ridiculed by my friends and family, but it found a way back into my life. I literally had no choice. It was April 2005, and I was on my fourth month living on my own in Los Angeles. I was finally making the transition from acting in theater to acting in TV and film professionally.

I had a morning acting class to go to that I loved. However, I woke up with the strongest gut feeling ever *not* to go to class. I couldn't place it at all, but I had this awful feeling that if I went to the class, something bad was going to happen. My mom was in town visiting me and she insisted that I go, and since I had no real reason outside of my gut feeling not to go, I started to get ready.

The apartment I lived in at the time was on Orchid Avenue, a quiet little street that dead-ended at the back wall of the famous Chinese Theater at the Hollywood & Highland Center. I lived in a building that had been constructed in the early 1920s Hollywoodland heyday. Like most small apartment buildings from that era, it had no parking (neither lot nor garage), only permitted (and extremely limited) street parking. This meant I often had to park my car many blocks away or up the steep hill that Orchid Avenue becomes after it crosses Franklin Avenue. This was the case on this fateful morning, just a few days before my seventeenth birthday.

Against everything in me that was *screaming* at me not to go to acting class, I finished getting ready and walked out the front door of my building. It was a *very* early morning acting class, and LA, the city where everyone loves to sleep late, was akin to a ghost town at that hour. As soon as I crossed the street, I was met by a very tall man who was carrying a knife, which he promptly shoved right up, lengthwise, against my abdomen. If he moved the knife (which was very sharp and very long) just a tenth of a millimeter closer, he would have easily sliced me open.

He started screaming about how he had just been released from prison that morning and showed me some sort of prison ID card with the hand that was not pressing the knife against me. This part is a little fuzzy since I was pretty sure this was the moment I was going to die. I knew he wanted money, which meant my wallet with my license and other important cards that I had inside. It didn't matter, but I was not thinking clearly. As he was yelling at me, I somehow deftly slid the hand that he had awkwardly shoved behind my back into my pocket and right into the fold of the wallet where I thankfully had a twenty-dollar bill.

Once I knew I had my fingers around it, I lied and told him I was just going for a walk and didn't have my wallet on me. He had me in a strange position and was constantly looking around for cops, as we were in broad daylight on a soon-to-be-busy street. I told him I had twenty dollars, which I produced. He seemed angry but not enough to stab me. He took the money and literally jogged across the street . . . and stopped right in front of my apartment building. Knowing I couldn't walk back in case he saw me and then knew where I lived (I was pretty sure he hadn't seen me walk out of the building), I made the decision to very quickly walk to my car, which was in the opposite direction of where he was and tucked around a corner, up the hill and out of his sight.

I got into my car and started hyperventilating. I drove through the foothills in a complete daze, knowing I couldn't go back to my apartment. But I was also way too shaken to go to my acting class. I called my coach and told him I had just been mugged and wouldn't be able to make it today. He was very sympathetic. I kept driving around Hollywood in circles, trying to figure out where to go. My mom wouldn't answer her cell.

Please do not ask me why I didn't go to the police or call the cops. Those of you who have been in similar situations will no doubt understand the fear and confusion that can overcome you in a situation like that—especially at age sixteen. Also, I felt like the situation was still ongoing as I was actively trying to get myself to a safe place far enough away from my apartment but not too far, because the only thing I wanted to do was run into my apartment and crawl into my bed and die.

I eventually found myself driving down Sunset Boulevard headed east toward Vine. That's when I saw a Borders bookstore. Suddenly, as if I was being directed, all of the panic disappeared and I knew I would be safe inside the bookstore. I parked in the lot and walked in, barely paying attention to my surroundings. I tried to figure out how long I would have to hang out here until my assailant would hopefully be gone from my street. Almost as if I was being led by a force higher than myself, I felt compelled to walk over to a bookshelf on the opposite side of the store . . . and there it was: THE BOOK. Sitting on the shelf, silently presenting itself to me, was a copy of *Excuse Me, Your Life Is Waiting*.

I looked up at the Universe (God?) and laughed: "OKAY! I GET IT!"

I bought the book, as well as the author's other two books that sat next to it, plus the *Excuse Me, Your Life Is Waiting Playbook*—a sort of workbook with exercises that expanded greatly on the original book. I drove home, not quite processing what was happening. I drove up Cahuenga Boulevard, and just after I crossed Hollywood Boulevard, I saw the most incredible thing (so help me, God, this is a true story): on the left side of the street were two cop cars parked next to a van that had seen better days. Pressed up against the van was a familiar face: the man who had mugged me.

He was being handcuffed and arrested!

I was now in more shock than before and full of relief. The odds of all of this happening were extremely rare. Los Angeles is one of the biggest and most populous cities in America, and even the Hollywood neighborhood was large enough that it was possible to never once run into your neighbor while running errands. I was a few miles from where this man had mugged me, and he was just about to be put into the police wagon when I drove by the scene of his arrest. Had I left the bookstore a minute earlier or a minute later, it is highly likely I would have never seen the man getting arrested, and I would not have felt the combined shock and relief I immediately felt.

I was home a minute later and told my mom everything that had happened. She told me I should start rereading the book, and I did. I felt that same feeling I had the first time I read it, just a year and a half earlier: comfort and excitement. I got tingly and my head buzzed in the best way possible. I took a break from reading a few hours later to go to Universal CityWalk with my mom for lunch at our then favorite restaurant, Cafe Tu Tu Tango.

I still have this memory etched into the fabric of my soul: as we headed back to the car after our lunch, the winds were blowing through the Universal Studios parking garage. It was so sunny outside, a perfect day weather-wise. It reminded me of the day my mom first handed me the book on our way to the islands. I remember thinking in this moment, "These are the winds of change. Everything is going to be different and better now." I was right. There was something magical for me connected to this book. In retrospect, the entire circumstance surrounding the book reappearing in my life may seem jarring to some. The reality is, I didn't get hurt in the mugging, and a series of insane and rapid events ended with the book back in my hands.

I got home and read the rest of the book straight through. I really homed in on the section about scripting, but I also realized that to script properly, I had to understand the basics of manifesting and the Law of Attraction, and not just as described in this one book. I wanted to understand and learn *all of it*, written or otherwise.

After that day almost every day included at least one trip to a bookstore, consuming every book on the topic of manifesting, New Thought, and anything related I could find. This continues to this day. I have found in the years since I really dove headfirst into scripting that much of what comes into your life, self-created or otherwise, comes down to one thing: permission. But not the kind you think.

PERMISSION TO BE SELFISH

Poor is the man whose pleasures depend on the permission of another.

MADONNA, "JUSTIFY MY LOVE"

You don't need any permission other than your own to be happy. You don't need anyone else's permission to be yourself. You don't need anyone else's permission to be selfish. See, that's the thing: being selfish is not a bad thing. If you're not happy, which means selfishly embracing your desires, dreams, goals, and wants, then how the heck are you going to make anyone else happy?

Love yourself enough to be selfish. The website Dictionary.com defines the word *selfish* as "devoted to or caring only for oneself; concerned primarily with one's own interests, benefits, welfare, etc., regardless of others." Merriam-Webster has a handy site where it lists words closely related to other words. Under the word *selfish*, we find synonyms such as *inner-directed* and *proud*. In the same dictionary, a synonym for *selfish* is listed as *self-loving*. Sure, those positive synonyms and related words are stacked up against words such as *conceited* and *egotistical,* but . . . so what?

It's time to embrace your selfish side and start being honest with yourself about what YOU want, not what others tell you that you want. If you are hung up on being selfish, or maybe you feel by being selfish you will deny others something, I'm going to say it again another way: *Love others enough to selfishly go after your goals, and love others enough to allow them to do the same.*

Michael Jordan, still considered one of the all-time greats of basketball, said one of my favorite quotes ever about being selfish: "To be successful you have to be selfish, or else you never achieve. And once you get to your highest level, then you have to be unselfish. Stay reachable. Stay in touch. Don't isolate." See what he said there? That's the key. You have to be selfish enough to reach and achieve your goals and dreams *so that you can then use the good you have acquired in your life to spread to others.*

When it comes to using scripting to create incredibly wonderful things in your life, you have to be selfish enough to admit (at least to yourself) what it is you truly want. Sometimes people will say something like, "But, but, but . . . I don't even know what I want!" That person is wrong. They know at least one thing that they want: *they want to know what they want.* And that is a great start. It counts. I refer to desires, dreams, goals, events you desire to happen, and so on collectively as "wants," which is synonymous with "desires." Knowing what your wants are is the first step in creating anything in your life—especially when it comes to learning how to script.

For the purposes of this book, there are some basic terms we need to know: *wants* (and their really cool big sister, *intentions*), *beliefs,* and *scripts/scripting.* All of these things are key to manifesting whatever it is you desire in your life. Even if you have read every book on positive thinking, self-help, New Thought, or whatever, it is vital for you to hang in there with me now, as I have some different takes on these overused terms. We are going somewhere that you have never been before when it comes to creating things in your life on purpose. This is manifesting on an entirely different level. Manifesting miracles—from small to big—is easier than you may realize.

My favorite definition of what a real miracle is comes from the book *The Miracle of a Definite Chief Aim* by (who else) Mitch Horowitz. Horowitz defines a miracle as "a favorable deviation from all reasonable expectancy, such as the realization of a cherished but remote goal."[1] So, if you create miracles in your life by manifesting them . . . What the heck do I mean by the word *manifesting*?

MASTER MANIFESTER

If you ask anyone with even a moderate interest in the Law of Attraction what *manifesting* means, they will tell you something along the lines of "creating something." *Manifesting* to me means "bringing forth into the physical world a wish, dream, or desire that begins in your mind." You manifest something using methods and tools like scripting.

What does *manifesting* mean according to the dictionary? Merriam-Webster defines it as "showing plainly" or "making evident or certain by showing or displaying." *Manifestation* is defined as "an occult phenomenon, specifically: materialization." This second definition is the one we are going to keep in mind for the rest of our adventure together.

You manifested this book into your hands. Did you buy it at a store? Online? Did a friend give it to you? Did you steal it? Like we talked about in the introduction, no matter how you got this book into your hands or onto your device, you manifested it into your reality. You manifested what you ate last night. Humans are manifesting machines, and we are always creating and bringing something into our reality— whether it is a thing or experience—*even if that experience is to sit around doing nothing.* (Hey, if that's what you wanted, good for you.)

I WANT YOU TO WANT

The first step in manifestation is knowing what your wants are. So, what are wants? What is the difference between a want and an intention? Does it even matter? Well, let's tackle each of these very important questions one at a time.

What Is a Want?

To script, you need to know what you want. A want is a desire, plain and simple, whether it is an experience, thing, place you want to travel to, type of person you want in your life, or way you want to feel. When it comes to wanting things, people often tend to focus, unknowingly, on the lack of the thing that they desire. *It is really important to keep your focus ON the thing that you want and OFF the reality of it not being there.*

This can be really difficult for people when they are just beginning. It can often be difficult for people when they have studied these types of things for decades. If either of these situations describes you, that is okay! Thankfully there are two simple things you can use to ensure that your focus is squarely on what you want: intentions and your Daily Want List.

Intentions

One of my favorite ways of making sure my wants are focused in the correct place is by turning them into intentions. Think about it. Saying, "I intend," packs a way-more-focused emotional punch than saying, "I want." Let's go through a few examples, and then you can try it for yourself.

Let's say that you really want (or need) tomorrow to be a really good day. You want to feel aligned, happy, and content. Grab a notebook or your computer (or tablet or even your phone's notepad app) and do this simple exercise:

1. Write down the following: "I want today to be a great day."
2. Stop for a moment and analyze how that makes you feel. Close your eyes and take a deep breath. Let it out and open your eyes.
3. Look at the statement and give it a rating from 1 to 10, with 10 being, "This feels really perfect!" For me, I'd rate that statement at about a 3 (*maybe* a 4 or 5 if I'm being generous).
4. Now write this: "I intend for today to be a great day."

5. Analyze how that statement makes you feel.

6. Rate that statement. For me, it feels more like an 8 or a 9.

See, the word *intention* has movement and momentum in it. It is focused squarely on you, and it is also like programming yourself to carry out the mission, as it were.

Let's say that you want (or need) a job interview to go really well. Close your eyes and say out loud, "I want my job interview to go well today." Now stop for a moment and analyze how it feels to say that. Then say out loud, "I intend for my interview to go really well today." See how much better that feels? Intending things is a really great way to get the focus and emotion of your want into the right place. This is a really important aspect of scripting, as you will easily learn.

In the spring of 2007—a few months before I *finally* figured out the magic formula to scripting—I was playing around with my Daily Want List. I started to shift away from writing "I want . . ." to "I intend . . ." and I noticed it made a difference right away. This leads us to our second way of making sure our wants are where they need to be.

Your Daily Want List

I learned early on in my journey into scripting that I needed a way to focus every morning on what it is that I wanted. This is where I discovered the magical power of a Mead "1-Subject Wide-Ruled 70-Sheet Spiral Notebook." These notebooks cost about a dollar and can be found at any local drugstore or office supply store. I also happen to love cheap black pens—manifesting amazing things into your life doesn't have to be expensive.

Nowadays I use the notepad on my laptop or a notebook—whatever is handy. Again, it's important not to overthink this part. Some people prefer notebooks, and some prefer just opening their laptop or tablet in the morning to make their list. Either way, I highly recommend that you do the following every single morning when you first start scripting. It is also a great thing to continue doing after you get the hang of scripting. It is a really simple way to focus first thing in the morning, and it takes less than five minutes.

Every morning, open your notebook or computer and

1. Write or type "Wants" at the top of the page, followed by the date (this is an important part of what will become your daily scripting ritual, so doing it with all of your exercises now will help you make it a habit).

2. Below that, write a list of your current wants, written out as intentions. I always try to aim for seven or more wants per day. It is okay to have more or less (we will get into the details of this later in the book). The main goal here is to do it every day. Make this a habit.

On pages 38 and 39 there are a couple of sample "Want Lists": a handwritten one from the spring of 2007 and another more recent one from my laptop.

Your Want List is going to change every day. Sometimes a certain want will stay on your list for a few days, weeks, or months. That is perfectly normal. Contrary to the method of using Want Lists as a means of keeping track—where the lister often ends up adding new wants to a single ongoing list every day, resulting in thousands of wants by the end of a few months—we are only using the Daily Want List as a focus tool. New day? New page. New Want List.

Oh, and always follow my "Rule of the Good Gut" when you make your Want List: *If a want doesn't feel good (or it's too loaded with emotional baggage, etc.), just don't write it down.*

We have other ways, through scripting, with which to easily manifest the more "charged" wants into our lives. Seriously, the Daily Want List is not mandatory, but it is helpful and therefore should not be stressful. Also, it should take five minutes or less! Some days I write three wants, other days I get on a roll and will blow past the five minutes and write fifty wants. I do this because with each want/intent I type out, I feel really good, and it carries me to realizing another want, and so on. This is not rocket science, despite what many will tell you.

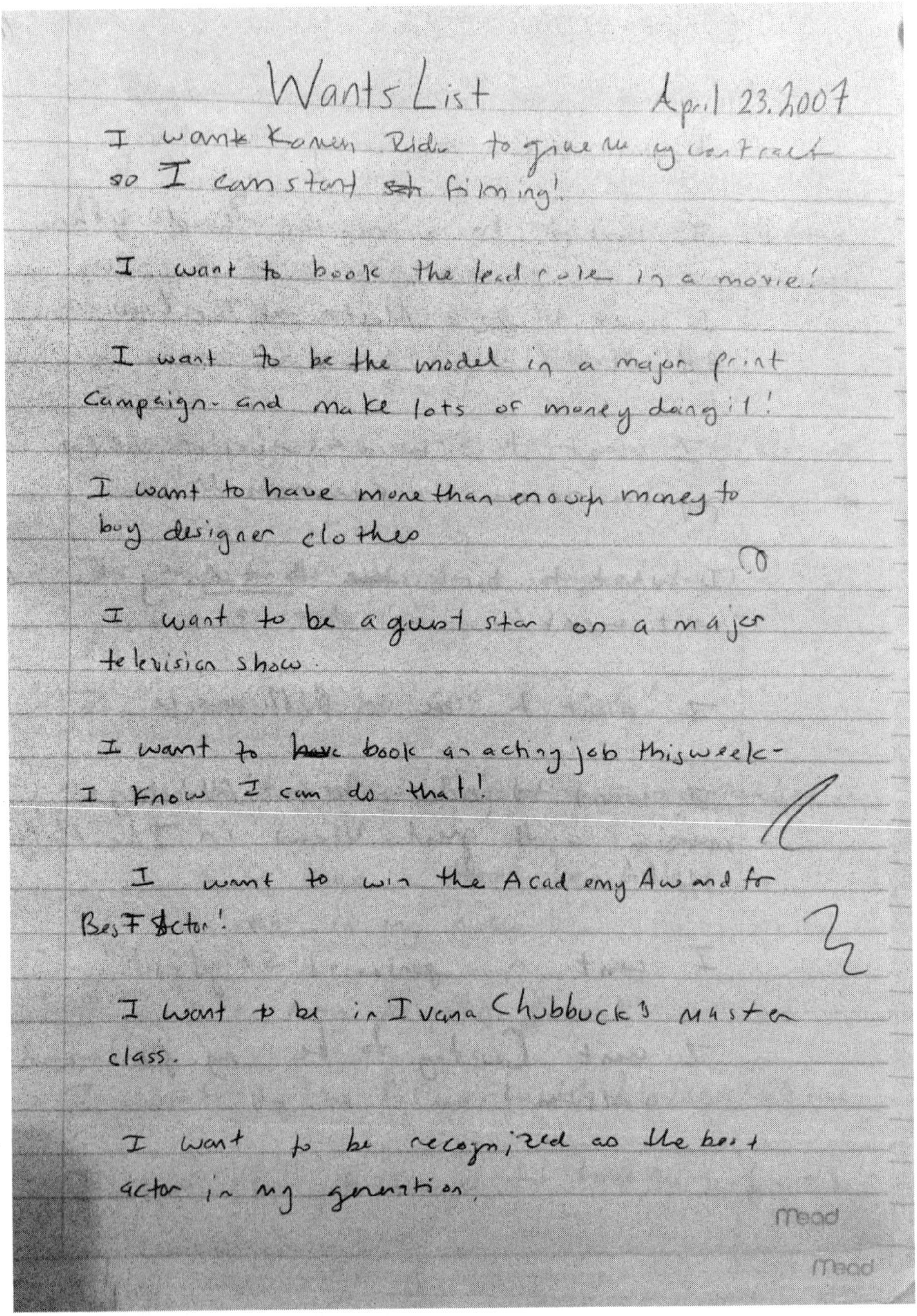

Wants List   April 23, 2007

I want Karen Ride to give me my contract so I can start set filming!

I want to book the lead role in a movie!

I want to be the model in a major print campaign- and make lots of money dang it!

I want to have more than enough money to buy designer clothes

I want to be a guest star on a major television show.

I want to book an acting job this week - I know I can do that!

I want to win the Academy Award for Best Actor!

I want to be in Ivana Chubbuck's master class.

I want to be recognized as the best actor in my generation.

Mead
Mead

Fig. 3.1. Handwritten Want List

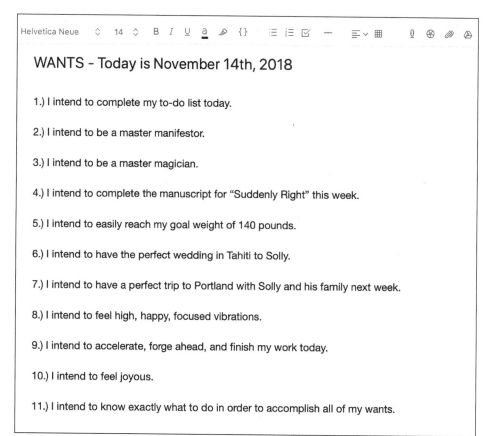

Fig. 3.2. Typed Want List

Beliefs and Knowing

One of the most interesting aspects of manifesting and creating is the importance of belief. It has been talked about and studied, and people around the world write books, papers, and articles espousing the importance of believing. But what does believing in something have to do with creating things in your reality? Belief is something that drives motivation and action. The power of scripting—real day-to-day scripting—is that we aren't creating in some nebulous future. We are only looking ahead to the next twelve hours or so, and that creates an entirely different framework in our minds.

Tim Knight, founder of Focus 3, writes on his website:

What you believe drives what you do, and what you do determines what you achieve. This is true everywhere in life: business, athletics, education, and personal relationships.

What you believe empowers you, or what you believe limits you. Empowering belief pulls your performance up; limiting belief pulls your performance down. This is especially true under competitive pressure or in response to challenging situations.

The good news is that what you believe is your choice. . . . The power of belief resides in its ability to do four things: Belief creates vision. Belief creates strength of will. Belief creates resilience. Belief ignites and activates.[2]

When it comes to belief, we often have so many conflicting things we believe that it can be tricky to reinforce specific beliefs—not only in your desires but also in your ability to use the tools we are learning to receive the things in life on your list. The key here is that we need to train our brains to see clearly that the processes laid out in this book *do* work. How do we do this if we have had a life where not much has worked when it comes to making dreams and desires come true? Well, this is one of my personal secret recipes for training your brain: always remember that the mundane is magical.

THE MAGIC OF THE MUNDANE

Every once in a while a friend or someone I am coaching will come to me feeling stuck with their manifestations after having had wonderful initial success. Every single time, without fail, the reason they have stopped having manifestations appear is because of one simple thing: they aren't writing things they consider "boring" or "trivial" on their Want List. Let me explain, and please bear with me here because this is one of the most crucial tips I can give you about manifesting. When you write your Daily Want List, there will inevitably be some things on there that you don't believe are possible for you to have or experience in your life yet—*and that's okay.* This is an important factor to consider when you are writing your Daily Want List.

The thing is, if you stick to the huge, massive intentions only (like marrying royalty and living in a castle or winning an Academy Award), after a few weeks or months of writing down *only* intentions like this, two things tend to happen: you stop feeling good when you write things down, and you aren't manifesting anything at all.

Now, before you start thinking, "Wait a minute, Royce! I thought you said I can have anything I desire!" hear me out, because *you can have everything you desire,* and you can have it really quickly with this one incredible tip that is going to sound really dull . . . until you start testing it out!

Here's the best thing about your Wants and your life in general as it pertains to bringing new things into your life: there is *always* going to be something you believe is likely, if not outright possible. Like going to the dentist. Don't laugh, because this isn't a random example. My partner Solly's best friend had hit a wall with her manifesting work. She called me, upset and angry at the universe. She asked me what she could to do to turn things around because, despite some initial success, her manifestations had come to a complete stop.

"When is your next checkup appointment with your dentist?" I asked her, dead serious.

After I assured her that I was serious, she told me that her next appointment happened to be the following week. I asked this because I remembered her saying that she likes dental appointments because they give her an excuse to leave work early and drive down a scenic road she rarely gets to see in her day-to-day life.

"Great!" I said. "Tell me about other normal stuff you're doing over the course of the next few days." I probed her for more information about her plans for the upcoming days. She told me that she planned to go grocery shopping on Sunday, and she had a dinner date with her parents the following Monday.

"Awesome! Starting tomorrow morning, when you're writing

your Want List, you are going to write at least two intentions relating to your dental appointment, and a few more that are about your dinner with your parents and your weekly grocery shopping. Make them things you know will happen. For example, write down that you intend to have an easy dental appointment, that you intend to buy those special organic apples you love, and that you intend to enjoy spending time with your parents' dog when you have dinner at their house."

"But, Royce, I'm not afraid of my dentist, so those appointments are always easy, I know I'm going to buy the apples, because I always buy them . . . and I love seeing my parents' dog. I don't understand how this is going to help me start manifesting easily again!"

I advised her to think of these "mundane" intentions as flexible items on her list that are in addition to the "big dream" intentions she had been writing. By *flexible,* I meant she could add more intentions of things she knows will almost absolutely happen over the coming days and weeks, and she could swap out having an easy time at the dentist's and perhaps intend to get a free sample of toothpaste instead (since her dentist always gives her one). She still thought I had lost it, but said she had nothing to lose by trying it out. I told her to trust me and call me in a week.

When she called, it had only been five days since we had spoken about adding in the magical mundane items to her daily Want List. She was elated. Not only had the obvious things we talked about (like buying the apples) manifested into her reality, but she told me how she also was asked out on a date while she was grocery shopping! Not only that, but a management position at her company opened up suddenly, and her boss asked her to come in to interview for the job, which would include a small raise.

So what happened? How did writing things down that she *knew* would happen already help "unstick" the manifestation of other, more exciting things on her Want List? There is actually some really cool science to help us understand, at least partially, what happened.

A SCIENTIFIC KEY TO MANIFESTATION

The first clue to our magical mundane Want List success can be found in a process carried out in our brain stem by a set of interconnected nuclei that make up what is known as the reticular formation.[3] The neurons in this area of your brain form incredibly complex networks and help control everything from our transitions between sleep and wakefulness to the amount of dopamine (your internal reward chemical) released into your system. But we are going to focus on just one aspect of your reticular formation for now: the extrathalamic control modulatory system, which you may have heard called the reticular activating system (RAS) by positive-thinking leaders such as Mel Robbins.

Based on years of research, I feel confident telling you that I personally believe the RAS is a key to manifestation. The coolest part, to me, is that the scientific studies of our RAS are leading many to believe that this formation the size of our little finger may be the key to how we create and bring things into our life! This may sound like woo-woo, but it isn't!

In a fascinating article titled "How Your Brain's Reticular Activating System (RAS) Determines Your Success," author Akshay Gupta explains how our reticular activating system acts like a filter for the billions of pieces of information that are being flung at our senses daily. He writes:

> It helps to think of the reticular activating system (RAS) as a gatekeeper of your brain. Its job is to sort through the massive amounts of information delivered to you by your sensory organs. Some of these stimulations always get through, for example hearing your name called. However, there is information that your brain can do without and the RAS makes the decision to dismiss it. Basically, the RAS lets in information that you are already focused on.[4]

Have you ever heard someone mention a somewhat uncommon word to you, like *Windsor,* or have you ever casually noticed a number, like 11:11, and then, seemingly out of nowhere, you start seeing the word *Windsor* and the number 11:11 almost everywhere? Contrary to superstition, this is actually your RAS at work! When you experience this, you are experiencing what is known as the Baader-Meinhof phenomenon. It turns out that this weirdness of suddenly seeing the same specific thing over and over isn't so weird at all thanks to new breakthroughs in neuroscientific research. What was once thought of in the scientific community as a phenomenon that had to be named but couldn't be explained is something for which we now know our RAS is responsible! Our RAS is what creates the Baader-Meinhof phenomenon in our experience. As the people at HowStuffWorks explain:

> This phenomenon occurs when the thing you've just noticed, experienced or been told about suddenly crops up constantly. It gives you the feeling that out of nowhere, pretty much everyone and their cousin are talking about the subject—or that it is swiftly surrounding you. And you're not crazy; you are totally seeing it more. But the thing is, of course, that's because you're noticing it more.[5]

There are a couple of different brain processes at play here. The first is *selective attention,* which occurs when you are intrigued by something new and become primed (subconsciously) to keep your senses open for it; you find that it occurs more often than you would consciously expect. The second is *confirmation bias,* which is when you interpret your first few sightings of that new thing as confirmation that that new thing is now *everywhere.*[6]

So why does this matter when we are talking about a list of intentions, desires, and beliefs? Well, our RAS is a filter that is programmed. I like to think of our brain as a computer that can be programmed with great apps and software . . . or infected with viruses that need cleaning. The good thing is that both of these are possible: programming and cleaning. All of the exercises in this book, including my personal method of scripting, at least in part help reprogram our mental computer and clean and re-focus our brain's filter.

Mel Robbins (who was the first person I had ever heard discuss the RAS) explained it best:

> [G]uess who programmed that filter? You did! And so did the people from your past. And so if you constantly feel like you're unlovable, guess what? Your reticular activating system is going through the day and it is going to point out every single piece of evidence that confirms that negative belief that you have. If you think that people don't like you at work, the Reticular Activating System, the filter, it is literally going to be looking for evidence to confirm that belief all day long.[7]

Our RAS decides what it lets through the filter based on the following two factors:

1. What *we* deem important (our goals and all the things we have reinforced over the years through belief).
2. Our survival, specifically what in the current moment will allow us to continue to stay alive. (This is because our RAS is hardwired to focus on our survival.)

That means that our RAS is focused on two main things—how important the information it is receiving is to our immediate survival and how important something is to us because *we* keep telling it to focus on something. That is the exciting or terrifying part, depending on how you choose to see it.

The good news is that you have the power to easily and gradually reprogram your RAS. While most teachers suggest visualizing or daydreaming about goals, I know from personal experience that it is just as crucial to give our RAS feedback and written instructions . . . which is why writing down seemingly mundane things (that you know are going to happen) on your Daily Want List is so important. When the mundane things manifest in your reality, your RAS begins to make new synapses and connections regarding your

Daily Want List and reality. Your brain's RAS immediately begins to understand two things:

1. When something goes onto this list, it is likely to happen in real life.
2. I better pay attention to whatever is on this list, because it is likely to happen in real life.

This is important, because your Daily Want List addresses the two jobs of our RAS: **survival** and **desire**. Our RAS is now paying extra attention whenever that list is created because it knows, from a survival standpoint, that what goes on that list happens. You are instructing your brain to start paying attention to everything around you that could help you receive the things on your Daily Want List . . . including your BIG intentions, dreams, and desires!

Gupta explains: "If you think about a point in your life that you want to reach (employment, travel, marriage), your RAS will detect that this is essential to your life and do a better job at focusing on these things."[8]

IF YOU VISUALIZE IT . . .

Scripting and things like your Daily Want List, as you will see, are, in many ways, a "waking visualization" or "wakeful meditation." Visualization has been studied and utilized by everyone from scientists to Olympians. The reason? It works—really, really well! And, in my experience with clients and students, scripting can be more powerful than standard visualization. Plus, for those who have a hard time visualizing images in their minds, these written exercises are fantastic ways to achieve similar (and *better*) results.

Mel Robbins sums up what everyone from doctors to academics have been saying for years when it comes to what we have learned about visualization:

Your brain doesn't know the difference between something that actually happened to you and the things you imagine that are happening to you. . . . Your brain, when you visualize, encodes it as a real memory. And that's important, because when you encode it as a real memory, it changes the filter system, that reticular activating system.[9]

Okay, that is very good information, but how do we ensure that our RAS doesn't start filtering out these important things when visualizing isn't working quickly enough? That is why I take it a step further, starting with the Daily Want List. We start showing our RAS, immediately, that our new routines and things like our Want List actually work—**right away.** The easiest way to achieve this is by including our magical mundane items alongside our other intentions, goals, and dreams.

The reward centers of our brain, which are also controlled by the same overarching structure as our RAS, will start sending the feel-good chemicals and signals out when you start seeing things you put on your Want List coming into your reality. So we are doing two things when writing boring things on our list:

1. We are training our brain and its RAS through showing it that, when we write down anything in this Daily Want List, it is important.
2. We are triggering the reward centers of our brain when we get excited about things—anything (even the boring!)—on our list appearing in our reality.

After a few days (it doesn't take long), these small, mundane things "coming true" forces the RAS to focus even *more* on our Daily Want list, because it now recognizes that whatever is put on that list is important *because those items listed come true!*

I prefer an easier nickname for the reticular activating system/extrathalamic control modulatory system when I need to quickly remind myself how to get back into my flow. I call it my ExtraCOM System, because it sounds like "extra communication," which is exactly what we are doing when we actively engage this incredible part of our brain: giving it extra communication so it knows what we want. I believe there are some truly magical spiritual bridges to be found between the science of this system of our brains and our understanding of the nature of reality from a spiritual perspective. If you're interested, the RAS is one of the main areas of study I would recommend researching. But let's get back into finishing your Daily Want List.

It really is as easy as adding some simple intentions to your Want List. You don't have to overthink it, or even make it about your upcoming dental appointment or the apples you always buy at the grocery store. Your list could be the following:

I intend for today to be a wonderful day.
I intend to go to bed on time at 9:00 p.m. tonight.
I intend to drink four bottles of water today.

Plainly, if you intend to drink four bottles of water today, and you put that on your Want List as an intention, you are likely to carry out that action for a number of reasons. We know that is true because of our magical ExtraCOM System! It also encourages you to start making simple actions that lead to big results.

If one of the big intentions on your Want List is to easily reach and maintain your goal body weight, then intending to drink more water and get on a regular sleep schedule are great add-on wants. These intentions are easy to achieve, and they also help to keep you motivated. Now, to clarify, this is NOT an action list—we will talk about those later. This is part of your Want List.

You can write this want down as "I intend to stay hydrated throughout my day and night" and accomplish the same outcome. A Want List is NOT a list of chores. You have to play around and find the wording that resonates with you. Throwing a few things onto your Want List that you believe are possible is a really fun manifesting hack.

Within days of switching my Daily Want List from wants to intents,

I was struck with the idea of following it up on the next page with a Belief List, or better yet, a *Knowing* List. It's really very simple. Every day, once you have written out your Want List, go to the next new, clean page in your notebook (or computer page, etc.) and write "Belief List" or "Knowing List" at the top with the day's date. Then choose between three and five of your wants from your Daily Want List and write or type them on the page. This is where the magic really starts cooking. You are going to pick the top few wants that are the most believable to you. For instance, if you have written, "I intend for dinner with my in-laws next week to be fun, enjoyable, and calm," then you would examine that want. Even if your relationship with your in-laws has had its shaky moments in the past, is it possible that you can have a good meal with them next week? Feel around in your gut. If it feels yucky, I wouldn't add it to your Belief List. If it *does* feel possible, ADD IT. You have one of two ways to write it, and both would sound a little funny if you said them out loud, because it isn't how we normally speak. If you want to, you *can* either write it in the present tense or past tense, so long as it feels real. However, in my example below, you will see written what I call "twisted present tense," since it is sort of a hybrid of present and past tense. For whatever reason, this is what I've found gives this list its juice and power! So, on your Belief List, you would write either:

> I believe that next week's dinner with my in-laws goes smoothly and is fun.

> or

> I know that dinner with my in-laws goes smoothly and is lots of fun.

As you get the hang of this, and as you begin scripting more and more, your Belief List will become much more fun. It will grow to include things that you once may not have thought possible. If publishing a book is a dream of yours, after a few weeks of scripting you may write something like the following on your Belief List:

I know that my book is published.

or

I know that editors love my book, and I am being offered a great book deal.

Some people may confuse the Belief List with affirmations, and that is understandable. But the key to the Belief List is that you *must believe that what you are writing is not only possible but also very likely, if not absolute.* Also, the key here is that your Belief List changes daily. That's not to say that you won't have some beliefs taking up residence on your daily list for days or weeks at a time, but your list is *daily.* Affirmation lists are fixed. Affirmations have a funny way of being repetitive and limiting. They can also force us into uncomfortable areas where we start focusing on the thing we don't want—which is something we, well, don't want.

A Belief List acts like a magic key to unlocking your inspired actions, which help move you toward receiving all of the things you want in your life. So, in summary, when it comes to scripting, there are two initial steps you are going to do daily: (1) your Daily Want List and (2) your Daily Belief (or Knowing) List.

Got it? Good. Let's move on to step two.

Four

Step Two:
Write Your Daily Script

An ounce of action is worth a ton of theory.
ATTRIBUTED TO RALPH WALDO EMERSON

THE MOMENT I KNEW I had figured "it" out is seared in my memory. It was thrilling in all senses of the word—somehow exciting, exhilarating, and terrifying all at the same time. I was only nineteen years old, and I felt like I had realized the secret to having everything I had ever wanted . . . but for real this time.

It was late spring of 2007, and I had become obsessed with scripting. I wanted to know how to make scripting work . . . not just some of the time, or half of the time, but all of the time. I tried every method out there that was even remotely close to scripting. Whether it was writing page after page of fantasy set months or years into the future or talking out loud to myself, I tried it. With every new method I tried, I would adapt it into my own version. I felt like I was hovering over a buried treasure with ten metal detectors blaring and no shovel. I knew I was close. I knew there was something there, but I couldn't get to the heart of it.

As it turned out, I was making things way too complicated. Which, looking back, was a blessing in disguise. My search for a method of scripting that worked 100 percent of the time hit a fever pitch. I was bound and determined that, no matter what, I was going to figure out how the hell this scripting worked. I read more than three hundred books on the Law of Attraction, visualization, positive thinking, New Thought, psychology, writing, and everything in between. I watched videos, I talked to every kind of person from New Age shop clerks to doctors and a priest to try to get to the answer.

But no matter where I turned or where I looked, I kept coming up dry. I kept searching and seeking in every possible realm, looking for someone else to have the answer. *Someone HAS to know,* I told myself. But no matter where I looked, I couldn't find anyone who really had the solution to making scripting work 100 percent of the time. At that moment in my life, I would have been happy if someone could point me to a place where it worked 65 percent of the time.

There was something so frustrating about finding a technique that was so powerful but worked only 50 percent of the time. I had days when I wished it never worked. I wished that it had only been a stupid one-time thing back in 2003 when it worked. But the odds were too high. I kept searching . . . only to come up dry.

Then one night I was with some like-minded friends who were also studying New Thought, and as I was lamenting to them about my quest for the right person, book, or whatever to give me the answer, my friend looked at me with a stare I will never forget and said, "It's you, Royce."

"Excuse me?" I asked, not quite understanding what she meant.

"It has to be you. You keep searching and looking for someone else to have the answer to making scripting work, yet you always turn up dry. It's you. You're the one who has to find the answer. No one else is going to find it. You've been studying manifesting since you were a kid. You probably already know the answer. Why don't you go back and look at your notebooks or something?"

A lightbulb went off in my head. She was right; I had years of notebooks I had used for my manifesting work, but I knew that wasn't where the answer was. Not in those notebooks full of lists and long-form scripts. Instead I got up and ran to my room. I looked at my bedside dresser, and there it was: my journal.

I had only been seriously keeping a journal at this point in time for a little more than a year, and I was sure that maybe if I read through some entries from when scripting worked, I would find the key. I thought that maybe if I could look at what else I did besides scripting on the days when the scripting worked, I would find something. I started reading. And then it hit me: I was holding the answer to what had amounted to years of questions in my hand. I flipped through my journal entries. The reason I had even decided to keep them was because I wanted a record of everything I did each day. I also kept them to have a record of the manifesting work I had done. But the answer wasn't *in* the journal entries. *The answer was the journal itself.*

"Holy shit," I stared at my journal in disbelief. I realized something so powerful, so life changing, and so simple, it almost made me fall on the floor.

"My journal entries need to match my script! My journal entries need to match!" I was practically squealing when my friends ran into my room. I probably looked like a mad scientist who had just made the discovery of a lifetime. I had been overthinking the whole process. We all had. Everyone who taught scripting had been missing the point the entire time.

Suddenly it was like I had downloaded the answer. I just knew the scripting key. I told my friends that scripting would never work 100 percent of the time if we were always scripting weeks, months, or years in the future—or not even in a set time period at all! That is the literal opposite of scripting's power. Yes, scripting like that could be used to get you into the feeling place of having whatever thing, person, or experience you wanted, but it could be so much more! *It could be a tool that worked daily*—with a huge margin of success. But the whole concept needed to be turned upside down, shaken out, and put back together. I knew that I finally had the formula to making scripting work every day, every time.

The next morning I woke up early and decided to try an experiment. I did my Daily Want List and Daily Belief List. Then I did something I had never done before in my manifesting notebook. I flipped the page and wrote "Script" at the top with the day's date to the left. It was May 24, 2007. I then proceeded to write a one-page script as if I was writing in my journal at the end of the night before bed.

I wrote in all of the little details I already knew were happening that day, like scene-study practice with my acting class partner. But I also added in what I wanted to happen. I scripted in my manager calling me to tell me that I booked the role on *Zoey 101,* the Nickelodeon sitcom for which I had auditioned the day before. I also added in that I got a screen test for a pilot I had worked on that had been picked up and they were doing some late recasting on, as well as some other details.

I had been writing in my little green journal every night right before I closed my eyes for almost a year, but I wanted to beat myself to the punch. So I wrote something that I felt was easy to believe would happen that day, peppered with some of my wants (like booking the TV role I had auditioned for the previous day). It felt so right. It was easy because I didn't have to force anything. I already had woken up at 9:00 a.m., so when I wrote that in my morning script, it felt real because it was real. Adding in the small details, I made myself feel what it would actually feel like writing these things later that night in my actual journal.

The day went on pretty much as normal, except I didn't get a call from my manager or agent about booking the job or getting a screen test. I didn't let it faze me. That night I wrote in my real journal the truth about what happened that day. The next morning I did the same exercise with my script. I adjusted it to fit the new day. Back then my schedule was pretty much the same: wake up, audition, coach for acting, eat, hang out with friends, repeat. I didn't repeat the same script every day. Instead I would script in the morning, pretending that I was writing in my journal and not my manifesting notebook. I would write out the whole day from the perspective of sitting in my bed at night and recounting the day, just like I had been doing for more than a year . . . except it was first thing in the morning. My one rule, which was obvious to me, was that my Nightly Journal—my real journal—always had to be factual and recount the day's actual events.

A few days went by, and then something magical happened. I didn't even realize it until I was writing in my real journal the night of May 30, 2007, just six days after my little scripting experiment started. I stared at my real journal in disbelief for a moment, then ran to get my morning manifesting notebook and flipped back a few pages to my entry from the first day of the experiment. I was blown away. The morning scripted entry from May 24 matched my real journal entry from May 30 almost to the letter! I was so excited I could barely contain myself.

Below, on the left, is the text from the morning script I wrote on May 24, and on the right is the text from my real journal on May 30 — just six days later.

Script—Thursday, May 24, 2007

Wow! Wahoo! Today was so so so good! I woke up around 9 a.m. and I was feeling so good about my audition yesterday for Zoey 101! I could just feel this "buzz" all over me! I showered and did my chakra clearing meditation. Then, I studied my lines for rehearsal with [my scene study partner]. I ended up going to her house to rehearse and while I was there I got a call from my manager, Nils! He told me I booked the role on Zoey 101!! I am over the moon excited and I film early next week! I went home + got two more calls about a screen test for the KRDK pilot and another show! I was so excited, I rushed to [my acting coach's house] and we coached for over an hour. Afterwards, to celebrate the job + mom being in town, her and I went out to eat + I'm home now working on lines for the auditions! So much good is happening. I am so grateful and excited! YES!

Wednesday, May 30, 2007

YES! YES to it all! OK! So, today is a wonderful, beautiful, perfect day in every way! So, I woke up this morning at 9:30 a.m. and I went to [my scene study partner]'s house to practice lines/I chakra cleared (half) this morning! Then, as I was leaving, I got a voice message from [my manager] telling me to call him back! So, I do, and it turns out I booked ZOEY 101! And I shoot on Monday! YES! So, then, he tells me that I have an audition for a great movie tomorrow! I called [my acting coach] + we worked for AN HOUR, and she made me feel so good and confident about myself + my work—she booked a job—a BIG job today—a movie starring alongside [a huge movie star]! SO, then [my manager] calls again and I have my screen test for [KRDK] on Tuesday! YES! I feel good about it! I called [the show's producers] + we are all going to work tomorrow together on my scene! Then, mom and I celebrated at Koji's, [went] into the hot tub, & here I am! Something REALLY big is coming and it's HUGE and it's MAGICAL and it just feels so . . . wonderful! I'm gonna book at least two more jobs this week! I swear it!

The similarities are stunning. I still get chills reading them! On pages 57 and 58 are photos of my manifesting notebook script and the page of my journal for comparison to the entries above. You'll have to excuse my grammar and use of smiley faces—I was nineteen and writing in my personal journal. I was also very excited, which I'm sure you understand.

I didn't know what I was more excited about: booking the role on the TV show or finally figuring out a way to script that actually seemed to work. It took a few more days (not weeks), but pretty soon, the most incredible thing happened: my morning scripts were lining up with my nighttime journal entries! It was unbelievable.

After playing with the day-to-day scripting for a few weeks, with literal magic happening almost daily, I had a question: "How far into the future could I reasonably 'push' scripting?" See, there were a lot of reasons that this scripting was working (which we will get into in the upcoming chapters), but I was only scripting about twelve or so hours into the future each day.

I was still writing my Daily Want List, which had some loftier goals and dreams that weren't as easy to put into the Daily Script. Also, a lead guest-starring role on a Disney Channel sitcom came up, and I wanted it more than anything else on earth. So I decided to try something in addition to my everyday script: a ten-day script, once a week.

That was when the true scripting breakthrough happened.

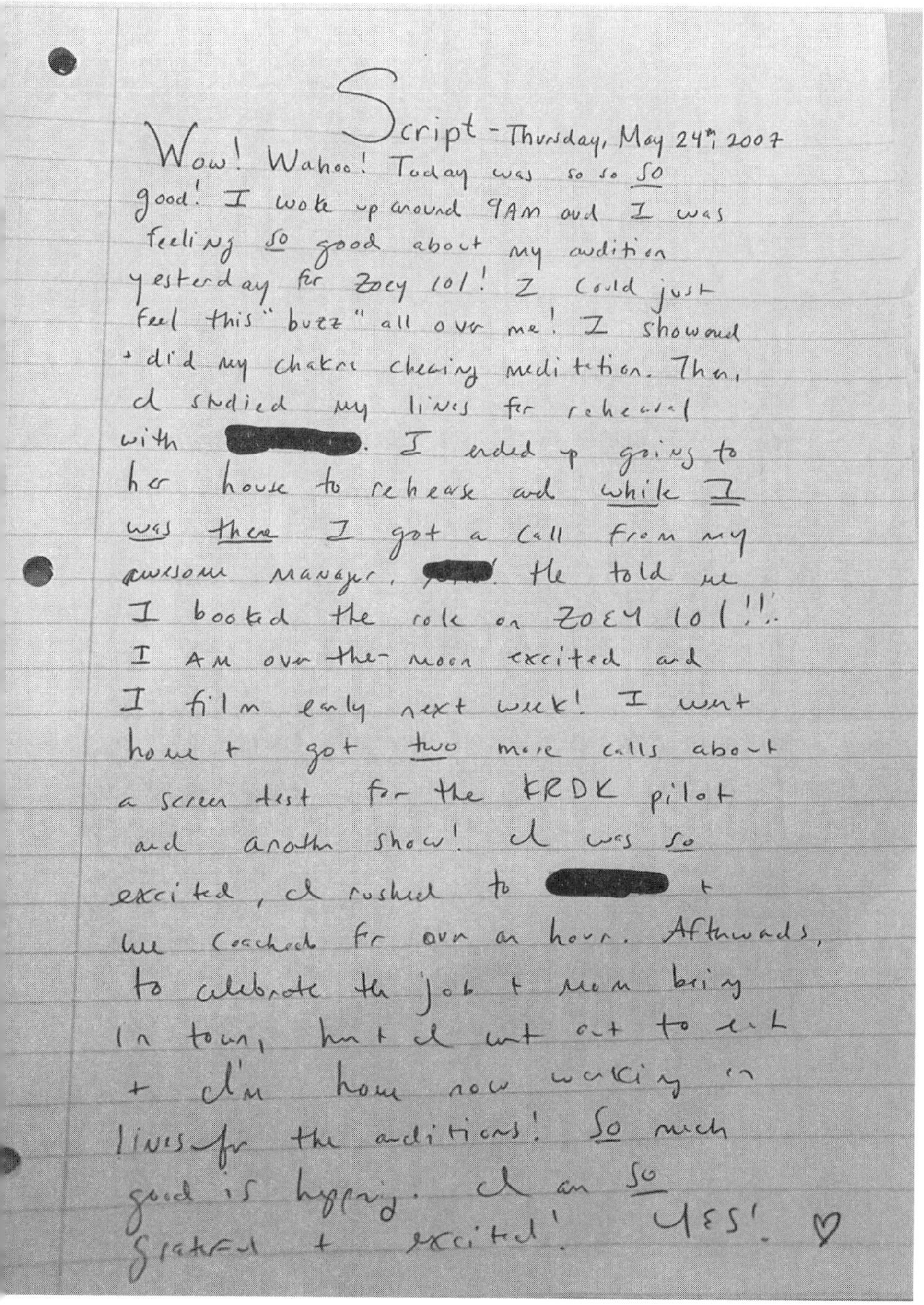

$\mathcal{S}$cript - Thursday, May 24ᵗʰ, 2007

Wow! Wahoo! Today was so so _SO_ good! I woke up around 9AM and I was feeling _so_ good about my audition yesterday for Zoey 101! I could just feel this "buzz" all over me! I showered + did my chakra clearing meditation. Then, I studied my lines for rehearsal with ████████. I ended up going to her house to rehearse and while I was there I got a call from my awesome manager, ████. He told me I booked the role on ZOEY 101!!! I AM over the moon excited and I film early next week! I went home + got _two_ more calls about a screen test for the KRDK pilot and another show! I was _so_ excited, I rushed to ██████ + he coached for over an hour. Afterwards, to celebrate the job + mom being in town, but I went out to eat + I'm home now working on lines for the auditions! _So_ much good is happing. I am _so_ grateful + excited! YES! ♡

Fig. 4.1. Handwritten script from the morning of May 24, 2007

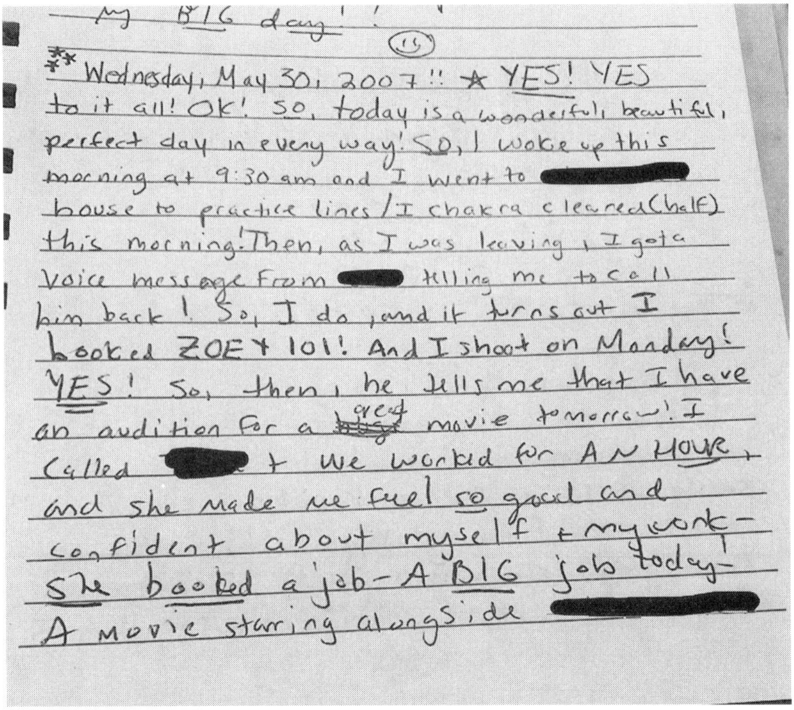

Fig. 4.2. Journal entry from the evening of May 30, 2007

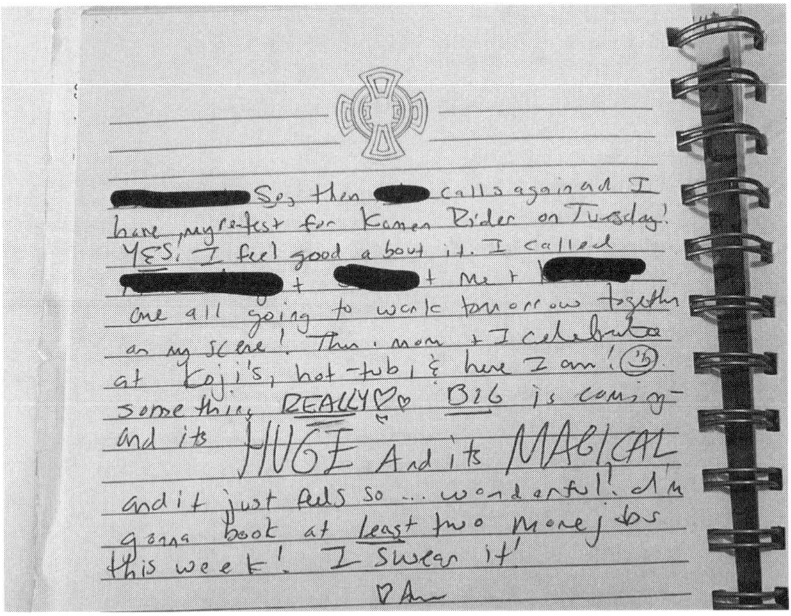

Five

Step Three:
The Powerful Ten-Day Script

Too much of a good thing can be wonderful.

MAE WEST

IF DISCOVERING THE WEIRDLY WONDERFUL POWER of the Daily Script was the crack in the glass ceiling I had been looking for, then the creation and implementation of the Ten-Day Script was the moment the glass ceiling shattered completely, and I realized I had broken through to the other side. The purpose of the Ten-Day Script is simple: it allows you to put your bigger and more exciting wants into your experience of creation.

Scripting as a whole, when done properly, is all about taking control of your life and circumstances. Scripting, at its core, is just as much about getting into the "feeling and focus place" of having your wants as it is about taking the reins back from the outside world. Your life is YOUR life, and you are now its sole writer, producer, and director.

So, if the Daily Scripts (scripting one page in the morning, writing in the real journal at night) were working so well, why did I feel the need to add in a second exercise? Well, as I mentioned in the previous chapter, I wanted a way to start fitting in some of the bigger desires from my Want List into my scripting work. And, to be honest, the

Ten-Day Script is not really a second exercise at all. You are not even really adding a thing to your weekly routine. What you are doing is changing how you script on Sunday.

Studies have shown that breaking up your daily routine has a positive effect on creating new habits. Scripting is a new habit you are forming. A popular myth is that it only takes twenty-one days to form a new habit. This has been scientifically proved to be untrue. It actually turns out that it takes a little more than two months (about sixty-six days). More interestingly, studies show that missing a day or breaking up the routine does not reset this scary "habit clock" that so many of us put in our minds when trying to accomplish some positive, permanent change in our lives . . . and that's a good thing!

Now, I'm not advocating taking breaks from your Daily Script— not at all! It is simple and fun—especially when you quickly see how things you write about in the morning are created just a few minutes or hours later in the same day. But we also want to create beyond our daily scripts, and that is where the Ten-Day Script comes into play.

The Ten-Day Script came about in a really funny way. It was actually a creation of my Daily Scripts, where I started scripting that I had found the perfect way to add my bigger, more long-term intentions and wants into my scripting work. This is a key to manifesting when you are stuck, by the way: *use what is working to create the solution to what is not working.* We will get into this near the close of the book, as it is an immensely powerful tool.

Anyway, as I was experiencing wonder after wonder happening with my Daily Script, I had already been going into auditions almost weekly for a couple of years at this point (early summer 2007) for roles on Disney Channel. By 2007, my meetings and casting sessions with the various Disney Channel people seemed to hit a fever pitch. There were casting directors for two shows at this point who were bringing me in to read for roles sometimes twice in one week. One show— *Hannah Montana,* starring Miley Cyrus—was already exploding into the mainstream.

The other show was new and had not aired yet, as it was just beginning to film. This was a show that went through many name changes, but the network finally settled on the name that everyone knows: *Wizards of Waverly Place*. By the summer of 2007, the awesome casting directors of the show, Ruth Lambert and Robert McGee, were calling me in to audition for various roles so often, I felt like I should move closer to the studio where the show filmed! One of my intentions on my Daily Want List for a few months had been to book the lead guest-starring role in *Wizards of Waverly Place*. Once I discovered Daily Scripts, I wanted to find a way to put into scripting what I felt would be a breakthrough for not only my career but also my manifesting work.

It hit me like a bolt of lightning one Monday evening after my weekly scene study class. The class was normally held on Sunday evenings but had been moved this particular week. It was about 9:00 p.m. when I got home, and I was thinking about how close I was coming to getting a role in a show on Disney. I was getting a lot of callbacks for roles or would get extremely close to booking a job where it would end up being between me and one other guy. I wanted to change that. So I sat down at my desk with my manifesting notebook, usually reserved for my daily morning scripting.

For whatever reason, I hadn't scripted that morning; it was one of the only mornings I had missed since I had discovered the power of the Daily Script. So I wrote the day's date at the top of the page next to the header "Script" like always, and then something came over me. I started writing differently from the way I normally did for a Daily Script. Since it was the end of the day, I couldn't put down what I wanted to happen for the day since it had already happened. Below is what I wrote.

Script—July 23, 2007

OK, wonderful life, you are—right now—going to be made aware of two perfect things! One is: you are wonderful, perfect, and ideal in every way. The perfection and beauty and bliss of you—my life— is golden and wonderful! And two: everything will be perfect now! Everything is wonderful now. All of you, my wonderful life, is changed and transformed into a majestic, highest-frequency-the-human-body-can-have [being]! You are now perfect life, and I am so excited and grateful!

Now this was very different from any sort of script I had ever written. I was talking directly to my *life*—or what some may call my "higher self." I was not scripting something that had already happened, but instead, I was commanding my life to understand something: it was perfect now. (This may sound silly, but before you overthink it, just know that I have perfected this method in the decade or so since, so hang in there!)

Anyway, I sat and looked at the page, *and then it hit me* . . . I looked at the calendar and counted ten days forward, and then right below the first script passage, I wrote out what the date would be ten days into the future: August 3, 2007. I could feel tingles buzzing all up and down my spine. I began to write as if it was ten days into the future, and I was writing one of my long journal entries looking back over these days. Now, for whatever reason, two amazing things flowed out of me right away: For the first page and a half of this Ten-Day Script, I only wrote about how high my vibrations felt, how wonderful I felt, and how positive the energy and world around me felt and acted as if I was saying this in that moment, ten days ahead in the future. Then, after I had really gotten into that great feeling place, I hit on the key phrase that would seal in the power of the Ten-Day Script: *It all started about a week and a half (or ten days) ago when I sat down at my desk to write a script.*

Those words are the "secret sauce" to the Ten-Day Script, my friends, and I have no idea where they came from or how I knew to write them, but, my goodness, did it change everything. There is a power in those words when you write them in the Ten-Day Script. When you are writing as if it is ten days in the future, you can sometimes feel like you are faking it, and it can feel a little weird—which is okay! But when you write, "It all started about ten days ago" or "It all started about a week and a half ago when I sat down to write my script," it immediately becomes this powerful thing that grounds you into the magic of scripting. This is what I call the "Ten-Day Script Power Punch Phrase."

From there, I just let it flow. Now, everyone has different ways of writing for different situations. I would never write the same way in my journal as I do when I am writing a book. My journal and manifesting binders are like fun letters to a friend (or my future self or whoever ends up reading them one day) and are very casual and goofy. That's my style, and I enjoy it. That is the reason that I try to match my scripts—whether Daily or Ten-Day—to my casual journal writing style. It also makes it feel much more real and believable (because it is!).

Now, after I wrote the magic Ten-Day Script Power Punch Phrase, I started going somewhat day by day, but I wasn't rigid. If it felt right to say something happened on that Monday, I wrote that it did (the same applied if I knew I had an appointment or meeting or whatever on a certain day within that ten-day period). It is important to know that you do NOT have to go through each and every day that make up the ten days. You are just writing free-flow, and the whole Ten-Day Script should be about six to seven pages of free-flow thought scripting (maaaybe eight pages if you are really feeling it, but you don't want to exhaust yourself).

I added into my script all sorts of awesome things from my Daily Want List. I put in that my manager called and told me that I had an audition for *Wizards of Waverly Place* without assigning it a certain day; I just wrote that it happened. I wrote that I got a callback "the next day" (without assigning a specific day) and then another callback. I wrote that I booked the job.

I added in tons of other details about my ten days that were realistic but also pushing the boundaries (in a positive way) of what I could include from my Want List. I was switching to a much larger, more prestigious talent agency that week (a result of my daily scripting), so I included that the meetings all went amazingly well. I wrote in some stuff about my family, friends, and home life. I covered all of my bases. It felt so good.

I closed my manifesting notebook and then crawled into my bed and watched some television for a few minutes. Then I pulled out my regular journal and wrote about my day as I did every night. This was July 23, 2007. On July 25—*not even a full forty-eight hours after I wrote my first-ever Ten-Day Script*—I got a call from my manager telling me that I had an audition for not just any role but for the lead guest star on *Wizards of Waverly Place*!

Now, if you aren't in "the business," here's a little secret most people don't know: actors will get called in for the same show numerous times for every kind of role—from one-liners to ten-episode arcs to full-time series' regular roles. On the same day, the same actor will audition for a Steven Spielberg movie and a soap opera. It really is that random and spread out. So the fact that this was not just an audition for *Wizards of Waverly Place* on Disney Channel but for a substantial role that was the top-billed lead guest star was such a confirmation for me of this Ten-Day Script. It was exactly what I had been manifesting and intending. Now it was time to bring it home.

I continued my Daily Script routine (morning script and Nightly Journal) every day that week. I wrote my Ten-Day Script on Monday. I got the call that I had the audition on that Wednesday. I went on the audition on Thursday, and I got a callback for the role on Friday that was scheduled for the following Monday. This left me with an interesting question to ponder: Do I rescript on August 3, exactly ten days from the original Ten-Day Script?

I was continuing my daily scripting, as usual, but I had this gut feeling that I should script again before my callback on Monday (which was July 30, if you are keeping track). This left me with Sunday night after class as the best option for doing my second Ten-Day Script. Another reason that I wanted to do the next script only about a week after my first Ten-Day Script was because I was having some issues with the relationship I was in at the time, and I wanted to add some extra power into healing that issue.

So, although it may seem a little strange to do a Ten-Day Script every seven days, it actually turned out to be the absolute best thing ever. I sat down after my class on July 29 (class was back to its normally scheduled Sunday evenings) and wrote out the date for the next day

(July 30, 2007) just to play around and see if that made any sort of noticeable difference. Then, as I did the week before, I wrote my kooky, kind-of-weird-but-it-worked "rah-rah" script/command to my life:

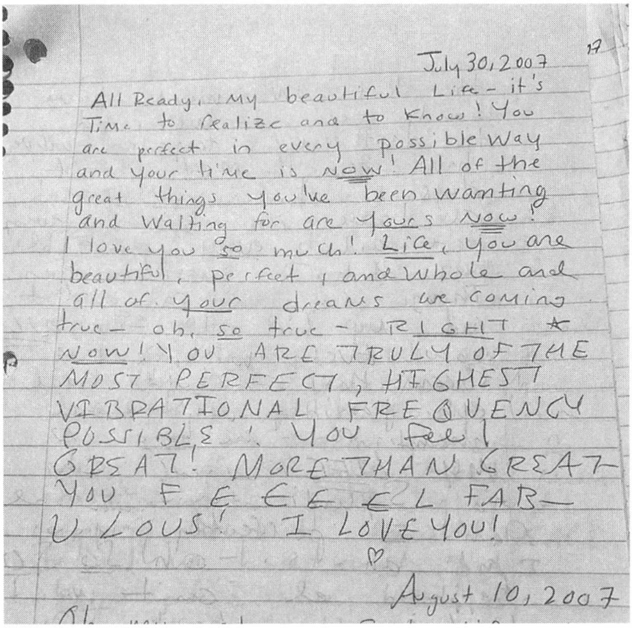
July 30, 2007

All Ready, My beautiful Life – it's Time to realize and to Know! You are perfect in every possible way and your time is NOW! All of the great things you've been wanting and waiting for are yours NOW! I love you so much! Life, you are beautiful, perfect, and whole and all of your dreams are coming true – oh, so true – RIGHT NOW! YOU ARE TRULY OF THE MOST PERFECT, HIGHEST VIBRATIONAL FREQUENCY POSSIBLE! YOU feel GREAT! MORE THAN GREAT – YOU F E E E L FAB-U LOUS! I LOVE YOU!

♡

August 10, 2007

Fig. 5.1. Ten-Day Script for July 30, 2007

As you can see from the photo, I then dated it August 10, 2007. Yes, I know this was eleven days into the future and not ten, but, again, I was playing around to see what worked. I figured since all of the adjustments so far to my routine had been positive, some small adjustments wouldn't be negative; they would hopefully only be positive. Plus, it felt really "right" in my gut to test it out this way, so I knew I would be just fine.

I started the portion of the script beneath the date ten days into the future with about a handwritten page and a half of general positivity about the past ten days or so, followed by the Power Punch Phrase. I wrote out all sorts of wonderful things that had "happened" over the week and a half. It was really fun to be doing another Ten-Day Script only seven days after my first one, because it allowed me to adjust things slightly to fit the narrative of things that had happened over the preceding week and also smooth out anything that I had put in the previous Ten-Day Script that either wasn't working or needed some pushing forward, energetically.

Now, mind you, I was nineteen, so this is cheesy stuff—but I'm a cheesy guy and writing like this made me smile. Over the years I've perfected my scripting and refined the opener a bit, and you'll find your own way of doing this easily. But I want you to see what the birth of the Ten-Day Script looked like. On page 67 is what the first page and a half under the date set into the future looked like. (I left the caps and weird spelling and grammar because scripting is about feeling and writing like you would in your journal and this, at the time, was how I would write in my journal when good stuff happened!)

August 10, 2007

Oh, my, oh my splendiferousness and fabulous life! Wow! I am just BUZZING—I mean BUZZING SO GOOD AND SO HIGH UP THERE! I MEAN IT WHEN I SAY the last two weeks have truly gone so well, and the last eleven days or twelve have been the most perfect days I have ever seen! I love my life in every facet and every possible way that I possibly can! Things are just so perfect and my life is so FULL now! Every wish, every dream that I could ever have possibly wished and dreamt for—are here IN MY LIFE NOW! Oh, I am so perfectly joyous and oh-so-oh SO SO happy! I can't wait to tell you about my gorgeous, magical, perfect experiences since class on the 29th of July! Ok, well, that week was already set to be perfect. I knew I had some great auditions and callbacks coming up and things were wonderful again with [my relationship]. That's where I will start! I went over to [my boyfriend]'s house that Sunday night after I scripted a perfect 7 pages and he was just so wonderful to me.

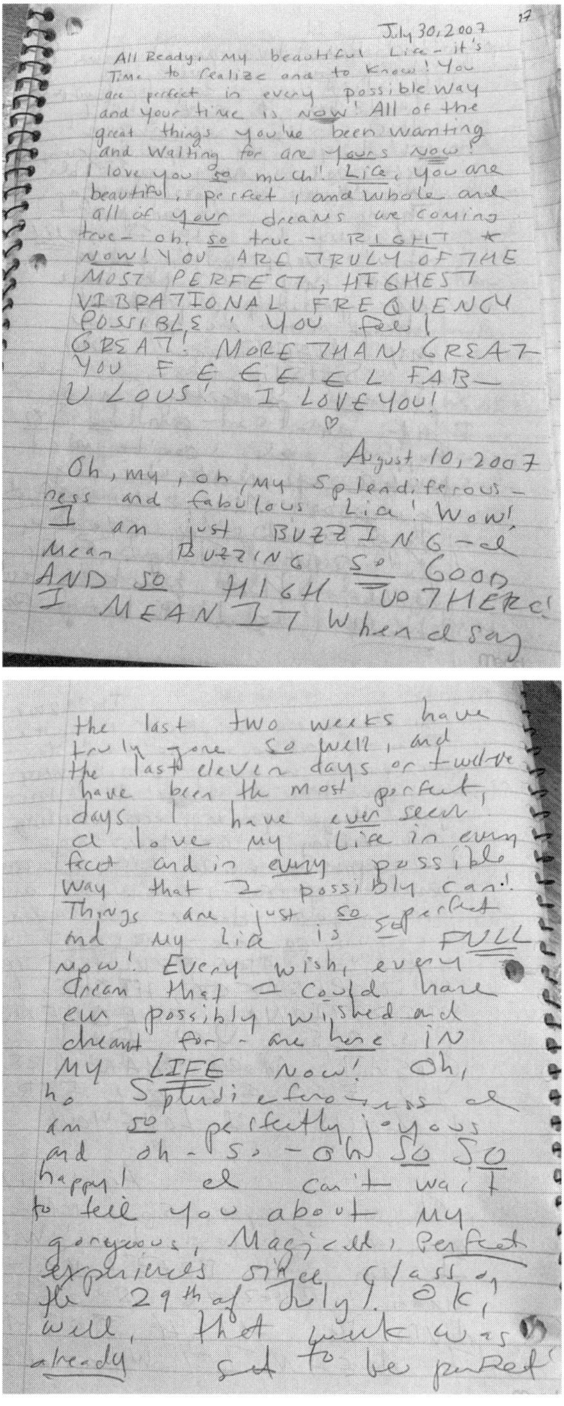

July 30, 2007

All Ready, my beautiful Lia – it's Time to realize and to know! You are perfect in every possible way and your time is NOW! All of the great things you've been wanting and waiting for are yours now! I love you so much! Lia, you are beautiful, perfect, and whole and all of your dreams are coming true – oh, so true – RIGHT NOW! YOU ARE TRULY OF THE MOST PERFECT, HIGHEST VIBRATIONAL FREQUENCY POSSIBLE! YOU feel GREAT! MORE THAN GREAT YOU FEEEEL FABULOUS! I LOVE YOU!

August 10, 2007

Oh, my, oh, my splendiferousness and fabulous Lia! Wow! I am just BUZZING – I mean BUZZING so GOOD AND SO HIGH UP THERE! I MEAN IT when I say

the last two weeks have truly gone so well, and the last eleven days or twelve have been the most perfect days I have ever seen! I love my Life in every facet and in every possible way that I possibly can! Things are just so perfect and my Life is so FULL now! Every wish, every dream that I could have ever possibly wished and dreamt for – are here IN MY LIFE NOW! Oh, ho Splendiferousness I am so perfectly joyous and oh-so-oh so so happy! I can't wait to tell you about my gorgeous, Magical, Perfect experiences since class on the 29th of July! Ok, well, that week was already set to be perfect

Fig. 5.2. The Ten-Day script

So this set up the script to then switch to a tone that was decidedly less Willy Wonka–sounding and more journal-like. But my point in showing you this is that it is really important to use the first page and a half of the forward portion of your Ten-Day Script to grease the wheels and really get your mind into a great place before you write the Power Punch Phrase, or the PPP. Once you put down the PPP, you are now officially altering time, and your future and this first page and a half of "rah, rah, rah" is important!

Below is a sample of what you could write that would work just as well for the first handwritten page and a half or so. (Don't stress over the length . . . it can be more, it can be less, but after years of testing, this seems to be the magical quantity to aim for, lengthwise.) And from there, you would carry on into writing about the events that unfolded over the past ten days. We will go into detail on what that looks like in the upcoming chapters.

November 6, 2024

Wow! I can't even begin to describe how amazing I feel in every possible way. I am smiling almost constantly, and my life experience is showing me moment by moment just how wonderfully high my vibrations are! Life is going so well for me right now and everything seems to have shifted to this sweet spot—it feels like my birthday and Christmas all at once! Everywhere I go, magic is happening. I go to bed feeling so, so, so good and I wake up feeling alive and full of positive energy. Everyone and everything around me is also operating on this amazing frequency—I can feel and see the joy emanating from all of it. I love how wonderful I feel—it really does feel great to feel great! This has been such an exciting week and a half or so, and SO MUCH GOOD has happened . . . I don't even know where to begin! It really all started about ten days ago—on October 27th—when I sat down and wrote an amazing 6+ page script!

Once I wrote the second Ten-Day Script that fateful Sunday night, the following week blew me away. The next day, I did my morning Daily Script. My callback for Disney Channel went exactly as I had scripted it—perfectly. I had never felt as confident about a reading for network executives as I did that wonderful Monday.

Tuesday I had two more auditions for two films, as well as private coaching. My relationship issues were also starting to magically heal. Then, on Wednesday, August 1, 2007, I booked exactly what I had scripted for: the lead guest-star role on Disney Channel's *Wizards of Waverly Place*!

So, to put that in perspective:

May 24, 2007: I create the art of the Daily Script.

July 23, 2007: I have my "bolt of lightning" hit to start doing a Ten-Day Script, which jumped ahead to August 3, 2007. I script about getting an audition for the lead guest-starring role on a Disney Channel sitcom.

July 25, 2007: I receive an audition for the lead guest-starring role on the Disney Channel sitcom *Wizards of Waverly Place*.

July 26, 2007: I audition for the role of Manny on *Wizards of Waverly Place*.

July 27, 2007: I get a call telling me that I have a callback for the role the following Monday.

July 29, 2007: I write my second Ten-Day Script—this time jumping to August 10, 2007—laying in more detail since so much more had happened.

July 30, 2007: I have my callback with Disney Channel.

August 1, 2007: I get the call that I have booked the lead guest-star role on the *Wizards of Waverly Place*.

August 3, 2007: I receive the full script for my first episode of *Wizards of Waverly Place*. (*This is the exact forward date that I had written for my first-ever Ten-Day Script!*)

August 6, 2007: I have my first day of rehearsals on set at the studio.

August 10, 2007: I tape my lead guest-star episode for *Wizards of Waverly Place* in front of a live studio audience that includes my family (who had flown out), acting coach, and friends. (*This is the exact forward date that I had written down for my second-ever Ten-Day Script!*)

So, literally, I scripted out my entire journey from not being on Disney Channel to being the lead guest star on one of their biggest hit sitcoms down to the *exact day* with the combo of daily scripting and my Ten-Day Script! (*One other fun side note to the freakiness of the dates listed above: the episode of* Wizards of Waverly Place *I starred in that I scripted about aired on July 20, 2008—almost exactly one year from the day I wrote my first Ten-Day Script—July 23, 2007!*)

Here are some pictures of me on the set of *Wizards of Waverly Place,* signing autographs after the first taping and being goofy with Selena Gomez and Jake T. Austin.

Fig. 5.3. Jake, me, and Selena

Fig. 5.4. Signing autographs

Fig. 5.5. Clowning around backstage

Now, could you imagine what would have happened if I had told any of them what I did to get there? At the time, I thought I would be laughed off set. But as I would find out very soon after, I wasn't the only one in Hollywood using New Thought and all of this so-called woo-woo stuff to help achieve dreams. But scripting? That was unique. And it worked so well, people began to notice something was up—and they wanted to know what my secret was.

I do want to pause for a second to address any skeptic out there saying, "Wait a minute! You were already living in LA! You had agents and a manager! You were auditioning for major studio movies and television shows and booking roles! Did you ever stop to think that maybe this all happened because of your talent and not your 'manifesting'?"

It's a valid question, but here's the thing: I know that I'm talented. But anyone who has ever even attempted to become a professional actor will tell you that talent doesn't mean squat in this industry. This is a business—a hard one. Also, *the entire reason I was in LA, having grown up in a New Jersey suburb of Philadelphia, was because of the manifesting tools and tricks I learned from my family as a young child.* So, yes, of course talent plays a role, but I coached sometimes five times a week, went to class, and still would only book maybe one out of every hundred or so auditions I went on.

I never let it get me down. I used the experience to hone my manifesting skills. I knew I was already doing the regular stuff right, so why not experiment with all of this Law of Attraction and positive thought business to see what sticks and works? Acting, though not conventional, is my life experience. So is directing documentaries, producing, and writing for major publications and media.

I realize this isn't a normal life, but it is my life, and I attribute being able to do the things I do to my work with New Thought. You have to write what you know, and since it is my truth, it is what I can give to my readers. The thing is, once I discovered the double whammy of the Daily Script and the Ten-Day Script, my career (and entire world) exploded open, and opportunities became plentiful where they once were not.

The only little thing bugging me at the time was *how the hell this was actually working*! Seriously, I was thrilled that scripting worked but also a little weirded out that it worked so well, every single time. But how? *Why?*

Six

Um . . . Why Does This Work?

Science is just magic that works.

KURT VONNEGUT, *CAT'S CRADLE*

SO HOW, AND MORE IMPORTANTLY why, does scripting work? The information in this chapter is not often found in books that talk about manifesting, positive thinking, or New Thought. This chapter is about science. One thing has always struck me when it comes to the world of manifesting and the world of science: While most students and teachers of New Thought/manifesting or creating your own reality eagerly embrace and search out scientific evidence that might back up their claims, the world of science has often heavily shielded itself from the ideas of New Thought; that is, until everything started falling apart in the scientific world. Now we have physicists and scientists producing papers in prestigious peer-reviewed journals such as *Nature* (arguably the most respected scientific peer-reviewed journal on the planet) and other publications with titles like the following:

"Physicists Provide Support for Retrocausal Quantum Theory in Which the Future Influences the Past"[1]
"In Spoken Word Recognition, the Future Predicts the Past"[2]
"Reality Doesn't Exist Until We Measure It: Quantum Experiment Confirms"[3]

And we find legitimate newspaper headlines like these:

"Is Our World a Simulation? Why Some Scientists Say It's More Likely Than Not"[4]

"Parallel Worlds Exist and Will Soon Be Testable, Expert Says"[5]

And perhaps my favorite:

"Are We Living in a Computer Simulation?"[6]

Umm . . . Excuse me, science? WHAT NOW? What is happening?

I am a researcher at heart—it is a strange hobby, I realize, but it has taken me to some fascinating places. It stems from growing up as an actor—we are literally taught to dive deeply into every aspect of a character and their world—and old habits are hard to break, especially when it is something so ingrained in the fabric of my being. This habit has naturally led me down a wonderful path of discovery over the years. Groundbreaking new facts, theories, and research on everything from the human mind to the concept of time have been testing our understanding of where the boundary between science and magic exists.

When I say "magic," I'm not talking about the occult or witchcraft. The word *magic* has been so misunderstood and abused that we need to look at the Oxford dictionary definition of the word to remember that it means "the power of apparently influencing events by using mysterious or supernatural forces." The dictionary goes on to define the adjective form of *magic* as "having or apparently having supernatural powers."

Notice that the word *supernatural* appears in both definitions. This is another misunderstood word that is often associated with scary movies and the occult. Once again, going back to basics is the best course of action when trying to understand a word. Merriam-Webster defines *supernatural* as "of or relating to an order of existence beyond the visible observable universe" or "departing from what is usual or normal especially so as to appear to transcend the laws of nature."

Let's look at that second definition for the word *supernatural* again and break it into two parts. First, "departing from what is usual or normal" indicates that something supernatural is something that we don't *expect* to see or experience in our everyday lives. Second, the most important part of the second definition reads, "so as to *appear* to transcend the laws of nature." This is where many people get confused. Something supernatural isn't actually transcending the laws of nature, it is just *appearing* to do so. That is a huge difference! Time and time again over the past few decades, science has shown us how things that appear to transcend the laws of nature actually work. It's just that over time we discover new (to us) laws, or we realize that we don't understand the laws that we so desperately tried to shove into place.

The first definition for *supernatural* above states that something supernatural relates to "an order of existence beyond the visible observable universe." That's the thing: we humans want so badly to believe that we know it all and have discovered everything that if we can't explain something, it's automatically considered unreal, a hoax, or a phantom.

But with the advent of artificial intelligence, quantum mechanics, memetics, and other groundbreaking sciences, we have had to face an either wildly exciting or cold and chilling (depending on your outlook) reality. We really have no clue what is going on around us when it comes to almost everything. NOT. A. CLUE.

That may seem like a flippant statement, but I'm not a scientist, just a huge fan and observer. I'm a curious person who is obsessed with researching where manifesting/New Thought and science intersect—and I'm not gonna lie; it gets pretty weird. That's why I will again tell you that, when it comes to science, you have to decide whether you believe in magic. But now we can use the dictionary definitions and create a better definition of the word *magic* for the purposes of this book.

Thanks to our friends at Oxford and Merriam-Webster, we can now say that the noun *magic* means: "The power of influencing events by using forces relating to an order of existence beyond the visible observable universe that transcend the currently understood laws of nature."

And we can define the adjective *magic* as: "Having or apparently having powers we don't yet understand that transcend the laws of nature as we currently understand them."

As you begin to implement scripting into your daily life, you are going to experience what others observing your life will likely call "magic." That is because, as you bring this simple, life-altering skill into your life, you will be creating and manifesting things that you may have once never thought possible. I will, in these few chapters, attempt to explain the currently understood science that helps to clarify what the heck is actually going on with scripting. This is a crucial and important key to the future of New Thought as a whole and to you also as someone using tools like scripting in your daily life.

I don't have all of the answers yet, and neither do the scientists, but I can promise you this: just like those few years and then months leading up to my discovering the key to understanding how to make scripting work, I am very close to finally nailing down the "how" of all of this. I'm not 100 percent there yet, but I'm hovering over it, and that's enough to write these few concise chapters. I know that my next book will be a deep dive into what we are about to quickly cover here.

Scripting and implementing things like the Daily Want List and Belief List work well. Not everyone cares about the mechanics of how or why it works. It's simple because it's magic. But all I mean when I say that scripting is magic is that in the act of scripting, we are accessing a power that can't *yet* be defined by the laws of nature as we currently understand them. New technologies and science emerge every single day that push the limits of what we once thought possible. As Arthur C. Clarke once said, "Any sufficiently advanced technology is indistinguishable from magic."

It really is all about you and if and how you apply these relatively easy methods in your life. I'm the first to admit that life sucks sometimes. For a lot of us, life sucks for years at a time. Even with knowing all that I know and being raised in a spiritual household that taught me the miracles of all this "create your own life" business, I've fallen off the path. I'm human, you're human, and shit happens. But I always got back in the saddle. Also, at times when things were going so well and 99.999 percent of the world would approve if I just let go of the saddle a little, I stayed on and determined. (I had to fall off a few hundred times before I learned that there IS no getting off the saddle once you get on.)

People have known for centuries that there is *something else* in the world affecting our lives. They first called it magic, then they called it the power of attraction. There are a lot of scientists out there who have figured pieces of it out and are slowly providing the science behind what we call magic. It is some pretty incredible stuff and, for me, it explains a lot of what we experience as magic and miracles. I also happen to be a science nerd and am obsessed not only with finding out why so much of this weird stuff works but also how we can improve it and make it work even better.

But here's the thing: when I sat down to write this book, I had to make a choice. A call, if you will. Would I take a true deep dive into the science behind all of this, as I have discovered it? Should I spend an extra hundred pages showing you all of the science I have researched thus far that supports all of the ingredients in the amazing bisque you are learning how to cook, eat, and enjoy? Should I show you where the vegetables are grown? What type of seed we used and why? Do you really need to know the acidity and alkalinity of the soil? The temperature of the sun at the moment we planted the seeds? Why the air, soil, and sun even cause the seed to sprout to make the vegetable in the first place? Or . . . do I just give you the ingredients and show you the science in another book? I landed on a compromise: I decided to give you the recipe to see if you like the soup and also give you a sampling of what makes this all possible, as I understand it.

I believe it is important to at least have a basic understanding of what makes scripting work so well, as it is very empowering. If you want a science textbook, this is not the place to end, but it is the place to start.

QUANTUM MECHANICS FOR DUMMIES

Follow your passion. Stay true to yourself. Never follow someone else's path unless you're in the woods and you're lost and you see a path. By all means, you should follow that.

ELLEN DEGENERES

I am pretty sure that I am about to melt half of my readers' minds in the next few pages. It's a lot to digest. I get it. But there is no reason to go easy and *not* rip off the Band-Aid, in my opinion. Before we jump in, I want to address something about science and New Thought: the current go-to "science for explaining the Law of Attraction" is quantum physics, and I'm sick of it.

We will get into quantum physics/mechanics lightly in a few pages because we have to, but for now, if you are new to this kind of information, prepare yourself: you are going to hear the term *quantum physics,* or *quantum mechanics,* used to explain literally everything in the positive thinking/New Thought/Law of Attraction world. Oh, and 99.99 percent of the time the phrase is being thrown around by someone who is—spoiler alert—not a quantum physicist! Shocker, I know. It's not that quantum physics doesn't have a place in all of this. It absolutely does. But what can be frustrating is the seeming willingness (or ignorance?) by many teachers to cherry-pick what applies and leave out what doesn't when it comes to quantum physics and manifesting.

As I've mentioned, I'm not a quantum physicist or a scientist, but I am a geek who likes to take years-long deep dives into these realms to try to better understand the world around us. So let's take a quick dip into the quantum mechanics field of study—without cherry picking.

First of all, you will often hear the terms *quantum physics* and *quantum mechanics* used separately; however it is now agreed upon by scientists that the two terms are interchangeable. So for our purposes, we will call it *quantum mechanics.* What, exactly, is quantum mechanics? An article on Live Science by Robert Coolman puts it best:

> Quantum mechanics is the branch of physics relating to the very small. It results in what may appear to be some very strange conclusions about the physical world. At the scale of atoms and electrons, many of the equations of classical mechanics, which describe how things move at everyday sizes and speeds, cease to be useful. In classical mechanics, objects exist in a specific place at a specific time. However, in quantum mechanics, objects instead exist in a haze of probability; they have a certain chance of being at point A, another chance of being at point B and so on.[7]

Okay, so in quantum mechanics, scientists study the very, very, very, very, very small. They look at things like subatomic particles and atoms, and they do experiments and research on them. Then, because nothing makes sense, and everyone is coming up with different results and theories, the scientists argue publicly with each other via peer-reviewed papers. Also, no one can totally agree on just what, exactly, is going on—just that something *is* going on.

The two topics you will hear about a lot when you first look into quantum mechanics are the "double-slit experiment" and "quantum entanglement," as both are popular subjects of teachers of New Thought and manifesting. You'll see why they tend to fit into the box of "See! This science backs up the Law of Attraction!"

THE DOUBLE-SLIT EXPERIMENT

The double-slit experiment is when scientists fire a particle at an otherwise solid wall that has two slits, or cuts, in it (see the figure on page 81).

Why do we care about a tiny electron being fired at a wall with two long holes in it? I'm so glad you asked! In a nutshell, the double-slit experiment (sometimes referred to as the "two slit") was first tested in the early 1800s by Thomas Young using light beams. Young found

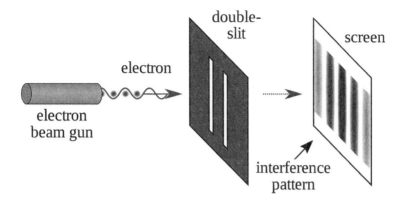

Fig. 6.1. Double-slit experiment
(image by NekoJaNekoJa and Johannes Kalliauer, CC-by-sa 4.0)

that when light was shot through the two slits, rather than forming an image of two lines on the wall behind it, the light produced a sort of interference pattern.

It was in the 1920s when Niels Bohr found that fundamental particles (in his case, electrons) also had wavelike properties, mimicking the results of the original experiment that used light. This experiment was furthered in the 1950s when David Bohm hypothesized that the quantum objects being observed through the beam were both waves *and* particles. Things got even weirder in the 1970s when scientists began firing one electron at a time toward the two slits. The single electron, rather than "choosing" which slit to go through, shocked scientists by still producing an interference pattern. *In other words, the single electron fired at the double slits somehow was going through both slits at the same time and producing an interference pattern.* The electron essentially passed through both slits and then interfered with itself.

While this may not sound exciting upon first hearing, it created one of the most intense debates in scientific history. What made this particular scientific debate interesting was that what was in debate was not *what* happened but *why* in the world(s) it was happening. Scientists were baffled because they could not explain this major thing: *The single particle was in two places at once.* If this was happening on the smallest level and scale, some argued, then was it possible that it was happening on every scale—even on our human level?

This idea opened the door for science to start seriously talking about the possibility of parallel universes. Yes, really. The initial experiments in the 1950s led to something called the "many-worlds theory."

THE MANY-WORLDS THEORY
FOR DUMMIES

Wikipedia has one of the easiest-to-understand descriptions of the many-worlds theory. It states:

> The many-worlds interpretation is an interpretation of quantum mechanics that asserts the objective reality of the universal wave function and denies the actuality of wave function collapse. *Many-worlds implies that all possible alternate histories and futures are real, each representing an actual "world" (or "universe"). In layman's terms, the hypothesis states there is a very large—perhaps infinite—number of universes, and everything that could possibly have happened in our past, but did not, has occurred in the past of some other universe or universes* [emphasis mine]. The theory is also referred to as MWI, the relative state formulation, the Everett interpretation, the theory of the universal wave function, many-universes interpretation, multiverse theory or just many-worlds.[8]

If this is your first time reading about this theory, I understand the need you may feel to take a deep breath. Hang in there; it gets stranger, but easier to swallow. A simple way to look at the many-worlds theory is to imagine sitting at a table with an orange and an apple in front of you. To keep this simple, we are going to say that you have two choices: eat the apple or eat the orange (in reality, there are millions of choices, ranging from not eating either fruit to cutting your hand when you go to slice the apple, but let's keep it relatively simple).

So let's say that the many-worlds theory is true for a moment. What this means for our example is that, though in *this,* your "current" reality (or time line or dimension), you choose to eat the apple, in another version that is actually happening at the same time, you choose to eat the orange. Now is where things get interesting. Let's say that in the dimension that you eat the orange, you discover that you had a long-hidden allergy to citrus. In that reality, you ended up going into anaphylactic shock and being rushed to the hospital. In the dimension where you ate the apple, you are still blissfully unaware of your long-hidden allergy to oranges. So in the "apple world," you go about your day as you normally would, while in the "orange world," you end up spending the night in the hospital, disrupting your weekly schedule.

You can walk this out as far as you want, but to keep it simple, let's say that in the orange world, things go back to being relatively normal for you—almost matching your apple world—except . . . they aren't a perfect match any longer. In one world you discovered you were allergic to oranges, and in the other you did not. This begins to create even more possibilities for other worlds. Perhaps in orange world you have a choice to go see a doctor to get a full allergy test. In one version of this world you choose to see the doctor. In another version, you choose not to see the doctor. See where this goes? Scientists who subscribe to the many-worlds theory formed from quantum mechanics believe that these parallel dimensions are all operating at once, hurtling forward in time.

THE COPENHAGEN INTERPRETATION AND CATS

The problem with the many-worlds theory is that it is just that—a theory. But it's a persistent one that scientists keep going back to when it comes to explaining quantum experiments. In the mid-1920s, when quantum study was getting into full swing, but before the many-worlds theory was put forth, something known as the "Copenhagen interpretation" was proposed.

Fig. 6.2. The Copenhagen interpretion
(image by Dhatfield, CC by-sa 3.0)

The Copenhagen interpretation of quantum mechanics was originally set forth by Bohr and fellow researcher Werner Heisenberg. It states that

> *physical systems generally do not have definite properties prior to being measured* [emphasis mine], and quantum mechanics can only predict the probabilities that measurements will produce certain results. The act of measurement affects the system, causing the set of probabilities to reduce to only one of the possible values immediately after the measurement. This feature is known as wave function collapse.[9]

Basically this often-taught method of quantum physics states that physical systems like electrons or light waves don't have defined properties *until they are measured*. This school of thought teaches that *the act of measuring affects the outcome*.

Critics of the Copenhagen interpretation included Einstein's friend Erwin Schrödinger. Schrödinger came up with a thought experiment called "Schrödinger's cat"[10] that was meant to show what he believed was the absurdity of the time's view of quantum mechanics. Many scientists did not like the idea of waves or particles being "clouds" until they were measured or observed, at which point the state of unknown collapses into reality.

Briefly, the thought experiment went like this: You put a cat, a flask of poison, and a radioactive source into a steel container with an internal Geiger counter to detect radiation. When radiation is detected, the flask shatters, releasing the poison and killing the cat. Schrödinger argued that the Copenhagen interpretation stated that the cat, for a period of time, is both dead and alive until you look at the cat. Once you do, the cat is either dead or alive, but not both at the same time.

THE OBSERVER EFFECT
AND ENTANGLED WONDERS

Schrödinger wasn't alone in his criticism of the Copenhagen interpretation, and something even more interesting was discovered and put forth by the theory's critics. Many scientists were not (and still are not) satisfied with the fact that many times during quantum experiments, it appears that the observer affects the outcome. This is known as the "observer effect."

In 1998 researchers at the Weizmann Institute conducted experiments under highly controlled circumstances that clearly showed that the *greater the amount of observation* on a beam of electrons, the greater the observer's *influence* on what happens.

A ScienceDaily article from the time sums it up well:

When a quantum "observer" is watching Quantum mechanics states that particles can also behave as waves. This can be true for electrons at the submicron level, i.e., at distances measuring less than one micron, or one thousandth of a millimeter. When behaving as waves, they can simultaneously pass through several openings in a barrier and then meet again at the other side of the barrier. This "meeting" is known as interference.

Strange as it may sound, interference can only occur when no one is watching. *Once an observer begins to watch the particles going through the openings, the picture changes dramatically: if a particle can be seen going through one opening, then it's clear it didn't go through another. In other words, when under observation, electrons are being "forced" to behave like particles and not like waves. Thus the mere act of observation affects the experimental findings* [emphasis mine].[11]

Another counterintuitive, scientifically provable, yet not understood phenomenon of quantum mechanics is what is known as "quantum entanglement." Quantum entanglement says that two particles, even if separated by billions of light-years of space, can affect a change in each other. If you do something to one particle, the other "entangled" particle reacts accordingly. In the 1960s, physicist John Bell proved that these changes can occur immediately—despite the seemingly improbable fact that they were somehow communicating or interacting much faster than the speed of light. Even Einstein, who proved that information can't travel faster than the speed of light, described quantum entanglement as "spooky action at a distance." (Side note: Einstein was not a huge fan of quantum theory. He knew something wasn't quite right. More on that in a bit.)

Experiments proving entanglement continue to this day. In 2015 alone, three different research groups tested the theory, and all three found support for the basic idea of quantum entanglement.[12] The problem with entanglement is that, like most of the quantum theories explained above, there are loopholes. Science doesn't like loopholes.

AND THEN . . .
EVERYTHING CHANGED (AGAIN)

If you've hung in this long for the science lesson, you're awesome! We are hitting the home stretch, so bear with me here. Now is where we introduce the most important part of all of this science as it relates to scripting: *the notion of time.* These days things move and change much faster than they did in the past century. In the same year (2015) that some groups of scientists were making sure that quantum entanglement held up in theory and experiment, another group of scientists studying entanglement made a rather shocking claim: *the future influences the past.* Okay, that is what the sensational headlines all read, but the headlines weren't that far off. Here is what happened.

The first study to come out was from a group of scientists at Chapman University who were trying to get a better handle on what the heck was making quantum entanglement possible.[13] As they studied and performed experiments, they posited that the *act* of a person measuring a particle can influence properties of that particle in the *past*, before the person even makes the choice to measure the particle in the first place.

Confusing? Not really . . . What the scientists discovered is that retrocausality is very possibly a part of quantum mechanics, specifically a key to quantum theory. What is retrocausality, you ask? In simple terms (for people like me), it is the opposite of what we grew up learning about cause and effect. Rather than there first being a cause, and then an effect of that cause as we were taught, retrocausality says that the effect can happen *before* its cause. It is the quantum equivalent of your body being in extreme pain today because you tripped and fell down a staircase tomorrow.

These scientists who put forth the idea that the future was influencing the past based their theory on "time symmetry." Time symmetry is a commonly accepted part of physics and science. It involves two separate but equal ideas when relating to physical processes:

1. Today is the same as tomorrow. (The conventional thinking being that if the laws that govern physics weren't the same tomorrow as they are today, it would be impossible to actually practice physics. But more on that in a moment.)
2. The future is the same as the past. (This is also known by the names "time symmetry," "T-symmetry," and "time reversal symmetry."

Time symmetry applies to most laws of physics, including those of Newton, Einstein, and basic quantum mechanics.)

The researchers explained that, if time symmetry is fact, then so is retrocausality.[14] Paul Ratner in his Big Think article explains the results of the experiment:

> The scientists describe an experiment where time symmetry would require processes to have the same probabilities, whether they go backwards or forward in time. But that would cause a contradiction if there was no retrocausality, as it requires these processes to have different probabilities. What the paper shows is that you can't have both concepts be true at the same time.
>
> Eliminating time symmetry would also get rid of some other sticky problems of quantum physics, like Einstein's discomfort with entanglement, which he described as "spooky action at a distance." He saw challenges to quantum theory in the idea that entangled or connected particles could instantly affect each other even at large distances. In fact, accepting retrocausality could allow for a reinterpretation of Bell tests that were used to show evidence of "spooky action." Instead, the tests could be supporting retrocausality.[15]

The same year that the Chapman University study came out, physicists from the Australian National University (ANU) were *also* able to prove that the future affects the past by replicating what was once thought to be impossible to replicate: Wheeler's delayed-choice experiment. John Archibald Wheeler's experiment sought to find out if the wave of light somehow "sensed" the apparatus in the double-slit experiment and adjusted to "fit" what state it ended up in or if it remained indeterminate (neither wave nor particle) until measured.

The brilliance of the Australian researchers was that they were able to use actual atoms (rather than particles) to conduct the experiment.

According to an article written by the researchers and published in *Nature,* this distinction is important:

> The only successful demonstration of Wheeler's ideas so far has been achieved with single photons. Here we use atoms, which is an important distinction, since atoms have many internal degrees of freedom. This allows coupling to the external environment through, for example, the atom's sensitivity to magnetic and electric fields. Moreover, an atom has significant mass, which allows strong coupling to gravitational fields. These interactions of the atom with its environment are required for the appearance of decoherence; thus, in this sense an atom can be thought of as a more classical particle than a photon. As such, our experiment tests Wheeler's ideas in a regime in which it has never been tested.[16]

The researchers ejected a group of helium atoms until there was only a single atom left. At that point, they did a (sort of) reverse double-slit experiment. They dropped the little helium atom through a "grate" of lasers, which scattered light in the way a solid grate would. As an article on the ANU website explains:

> A second light grating to recombine the paths was randomly added, which led to constructive or destructive interference as if the atom had travelled both paths. When the second light grating was not added, no interference was observed as if the atom chose only one path. *However, the random number determining whether the grating was added was only generated after the atom had passed through the crossroads.*
>
> *If one chooses to believe that the atom really did take a particular path or paths then one has to accept that a future measurement is affecting the atom's past,* [emphasis mine] said [Associate Professor Andrew] Truscott. "The atoms did not travel from A to B. It was only when they were measured at the end of the journey that their wave-like or particle-like behavior was brought into existence," he said.[17]

THE FUTURE AFFECTS THE PAST

As I was writing this book, some even more mind-boggling statements that I believe apply to understanding scripting erupted into the mainstream.

First, the *Journal of Neuroscience* made public a finding by a group of neuroscientists (read: nonphysicists!) that stated plainly in the title: "In Spoken Word Recognition the Future Predicts the Past." While most people who study the brain know that prior speech influences how we predict what is going to happen, the idea that our brains are pulling information from the future is incredible.

Using powerful MEG (magnetoencephalography) machines, the study tested fifty people and found that their brains were picking up on sounds not yet spoken: "These findings provide evidence that *future input determines the perception of earlier speech sounds* [emphasis mine] by maintaining sensory features until they can be integrated with top-down lexical information."[18]

In scripting, something magical happens that can't yet be totally quantified or explained by classical physics or science. However physics and quantum mechanics, specifically their findings over the past few years, have begun to shed some light on what may be happening when we write out our day as if it has already happened. Are we, perhaps briefly, stepping into the future to dictate to our past what we want to happen? Or is it possible that scripting this way gives us another clue into the nature of reality—that not everything is as it seems?

Once you start to notice your Nightly Journal and Daily Script lining up and becoming indistinguishable from one another, you will begin to understand why time itself is such a fascinating subject for me. Quantum mechanics—and physics in general—is currently going through a massive shift and identity crisis of sorts. In the middle of 2018, Quanta Magazine's Robbert Dijkgraaf wrote a stunning headline. It read "There Are No Laws of Physics. There's Only the Landscape."

You have no doubt heard of the search for the "Theory of Everything," or TOE. It has been a search by scientists who want to fully understand why quantum mechanics seems to constantly defy all conventional logic and understanding. The M-theory—a massive string theory—leads the pack as the top contender for TOE, but it's not the clear winner. M-theory states that particles like photons and electrons aren't actual points or pieces like we imagine them in our minds but instead are massive, long things that more closely resemble strings. This, some believe, is why quantum entanglement is possible; that is, it may not be two separate particles interacting at all, but instead those "two" particles may be one long "string." But the science is imperfect.

Dijkgraaf writes:

In string theory, certain features of physics that we usually would consider laws of nature—such as specific particles and forces—are in fact solutions. They are determined by the shape and size of hidden extra dimensions. The space of all of these solutions is often referred to as "the landscape," but that is a wild understatement. Even the most awe-inspiring mountain vistas pale in comparison with the immensity of this space. Although its geography is only marginally understood, we know it has continents of huge dimensions. One of the most tantalizing features is that possibly everything is connected—that is, every two models are connected by an unbroken path. *By shaking the universe hard enough, we would be able to move from one possible world to another, changing what we consider the immutable laws of nature and the special combination of elementary particles that make up reality* [emphasis mine].

But how do we explore the vast landscape of physical models of the universe that might easily have hundreds of dimensions? It's helpful to visualize the landscape as a largely undeveloped wilderness, most of it hidden under thick layers of intractable complexity. Only at the very edges do we find habitable places. In these outposts, life is simple and good. Here we find the basic models that we fully understand. They are of little value in describing the real world, but serve as convenient starting points to explore the local neighborhood.[19]

Dijkgraaf goes on to suppose that two people, Alice and Bob, are asked to prepare their favorite meal—Alice likes Chinese and Bob likes Italian. Both carefully follow their respective recipes, but when they pull their food out of the oven, the two meals are identical. At this point, Bob and Alice would most likely have an existential crisis, and this is a good analogy of how many physicists currently feel.[20]

But not all is lost. Using his wilderness example, Dijkgraaf explains that, as you trek further and further out, it becomes clear that there are larger, interconnected systems at play. This allows us to posit that there are two alternative recipes for the same underlying physics. These are called dual models, and their relationship is a duality. In essence, this means that the translation of the recipes' final outcome is just that—a translation between Chinese and Italian.

So what this all boils down to for Dijkgraaf is that one of two possibilities is true: either (1) *all* of these theories are connected, and "one large continent" rather than many islands exists, or (2) everything in quantum physics needs to be thrown out and a radical new framework discovered that explains all of this in a much better way.[21]

Remember when I mentioned earlier that I hate how people cherry-pick quantum physics facts and bend them to shape their view of the Law of Attraction/New Thought/spirituality and then spent ten pages explaining the long version to you? Well, here is the one fact that they all seem to leave out: *not once has an experiment in quantum mechanics proved that quantum mechanics theories apply to anything above the very, very tiny level (i.e., photons, atoms, electrons, etc.).* With that said, there also hasn't been any proof that the experiments done on a quantum scale *don't* apply to larger organisms, like humans.

So, in late 2018, an article published in *Wired* broke into the mainstream the news that a new thought experiment had everyone in quantum science talking. Daniela Frauchiger and Renato Renner (from the Swiss Federal Institute of Technology, Zurich) designed the thought experiment to question if any of the quantum theories actually hold up—not just in the macro scale (animals, humans, larger objects) but also at the quantum level itself.

The *Wired* article explains:

> Despite this lack of empirical evidence, physicists think that quantum mechanics can be used to describe systems at all scales—meaning it's universal. To test this assertion, Frauchiger and Renner came up with their thought experiment, which is an extension of something the physicist Eugene Wigner first dreamed up in the 1960s. The new experiment shows that, in a quantum world, two people can end up disagreeing about a seemingly irrefutable result, such as the outcome of a coin toss, suggesting something is amiss with the assumptions we make about quantum reality.[22]

This new thought experiment involves Alice and Bob and their friends who are now testing the outcome of a coin toss. Basically they show that if Alice and her friend along with Bob and his friend are all testing the results of one coin toss, where for Bob's friend heads is yes, and for Alice's friend heads is no, then Bob and Alice and their friends should always be able to infer what the other's answer is (Bob would know if the coin came up heads, that his answer is yes and Alice's is no).[23]

> But Frauchiger and Renner showed that in $1/12$ of the cases both Alice and Bob will get a YES in the same run of the experiment, causing them to disagree about whether Alice's friend got a heads or a tails. "So, both of them are talking about the past event, and they are both sure what it was, but their statements are exactly opposite," Renner said. "And that's the contradiction. That shows something must be wrong."[24]

The article goes on to explain that many physicists and researchers who, just a year or two ago, would take this thought experiment's results as more proof of the many-worlds theory, are now questioning whether the theories on quantum mechanics are universal.[25]

Matthew Leifer, the scientist who headed the Chapman University experiment postulating that time is retrocausative and showing that the future affects the past, is quoted in the same article (two years after his initial paper was released), which states:

> Leifer, for his part, is holding out for something new. "I think the correct interpretation of quantum mechanics is none of the above," he said. He likens the current situation with quantum mechanics to the time before Einstein came up with his special theory of relativity.
>
> Experimentalists had found no sign of the "luminiferous ether"— the medium through which light waves were thought to propagate in a Newtonian universe. Einstein argued that there is no ether. Instead he showed that space and time are malleable. "Pre-Einstein I couldn't have told you that it was the structure of space and time that was going to change," Leifer said. Quantum mechanics is in a similar situation now, he thinks. "It's likely that we are making some implicit assumption about the way the world has to be that just isn't true," he said. "Once we change that, once we modify that assumption, everything would suddenly fall into place. That's kind of the hope. Anybody who is skeptical of all interpretations of quantum mechanics must be thinking something like this. Can I tell you what's a plausible candidate for such an assumption? Well, if I could, I would just be working on that theory."[26]

BREAK ON THROUGH
(TO THE OTHER SIDE)

While it is clear that quantum mechanics is on the verge of a massive breakthrough, it does not discount how far it has come in the past century. One thing that physics makes abundantly clear is that everything is information, and information itself is computational by nature. And what are our brains?

The best current analogy for our brains is to look at them like they are giant information-processing machines, magnificent biological miracle computers that are processing massive quantities of information twenty-four hours a day, every day we are alive. Does this mean they are perfect at processing information? No. We know, for instance, that our brain filters and throws away most of what it is receiving so as not to overload your "motherboard" system. We learned about this partially when we talked about the brain's reticular activating system earlier in this book. That is just *one* processing component in the super computer that is our brain.

While our brains process information they receive like smell, taste, touch, and sound seemingly flawlessly, one thing that science is *not* so sure our brains process correctly is time. Yes, time. Here's a fun fact they didn't teach you in school: Did you know that the most commonly accepted view of time is something called the "block universe theory"? This theory, based largely on Einstein's theory of relativity, says that the past, present, and future all exist at the same time.

While we see and experience time as linear, marching forward in one direction, the block universe theory, or the block, utilizes the other most commonly accepted principle of time, which we talked about above: time symmetry. The block is not as confusing as it sounds. Basically every moment, including your birth and death, already exist in the block. The block consists of four dimensions: three spatial dimensions—height, width, and length—and one temporal dimension—time.

Dr. Kristie Miller, the joint director for Centre for Time at the University of Sydney, explains the block in an article published on the Australian Broadcasting Corporation website:

Let's make it easier, by visualizing the block model of our world as a three-dimensional rectangle, or cuboid. Two of that cuboid's dimensions (let's say height and width) represent two of the universe's three spatial dimensions. The third spatial dimension in the above diagram is left out—the length of the cuboid—and replace it with time. At one end of the cuboid is the big bang. At the other is the very last moment of the universe. Maybe it's a big crunch. The cuboid is filled with every event that ever happens. Where these events are in the cuboid represents their location in space-time. All events, including your birth and death, and this very moment as you read these words, exist somewhere in the block.[27]

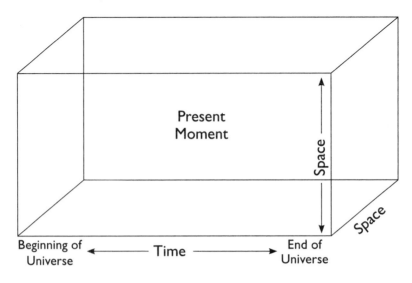

Fig. 6.3. A depiction of the block universe theory

The block universe theory is fascinating because the scientists who believe this theory (and there are many) also know this means that time travel is possible without a "grandfather paradox" crisis. The grandfather paradox is the old sci-fi time-travel storyline where someone goes back in time, and say, kills their grandfather, thus altering their own time line to the point where they never existed because their grandfather wasn't around to have a child with their grandmother. The block universe theory doesn't allow for a contradiction. This means that if you travel to the past, you were always part of the past.

As Dr. Miller explains in her article:

What will happen if I travel to the past? I'll get out of my time machine and start walking around. I'll breathe the air and chat to people. Obviously, this will have effects on the time I travel to. I'll tread on ants; I'll talk to people from that time; I'll pat horses, and feed donkeys and so on.

I'll act, in the past, in the sorts of ways I act in the present. But I won't be changing the past. Just as when I eat cornflakes instead of toast tomorrow I am not changing the future, I'm just making the future the way it is; when I travel to the past I don't change it, I just make it the way it is, and always has been.[28]

It's pretty wild stuff, and in recent years, a lot of cosmologists have been trying to figure out just how reliable the block universe theory is at all. One cosmologist—Marina Cortês of the Royal Observatory, Edinburgh—and other scientists are beginning to publicly challenge the block universe theory. Marina jokingly says that physicists may be spending a little too much time in their offices, forgetting that most humans are out in the world experiencing time in a forward, linear fashion.

An article on Plus Magazine explains Cortês and her partner Lee Smolin's developing time model:

> In their model, the most fundamental description of the Universe is as an *energetic causal set*. And rather than starting from a continuous spacetime, as in Einstein's general theory of relativity, Cortês and Smolin's picture starts from discrete "atoms" of time: "like the ticks of the clock."
>
> Think of the process of you reading this article and dramatically slow down time until you get to a series of individual photons of light from the screen interacting with your retina. Each of these interactions is an instance of time in Cortês' model, and each instant has an associated energy and momentum. These instances are discrete, but when you zoom out they appear to merge into a continuous passage of time. The future hasn't happened yet, and the past, those instances of time that no longer interact with any others, effectively doesn't exist.[29]

It's another interesting theory, but it is just that—another theory. One thing I believe Cortês questions accurately when it comes to time symmetry and the block universe theory is that if the block theory is true, what does that mean for free will? The short answer is that if the block universe theory were true, we would have no free will, because everything—literally everything—has already happened. It is the extreme of Determinism, "a philosophical belief that all events are determined completely by previously existing causes."[30] It makes you want to crawl into bed forever, doesn't it? There is a newer version of the theory called the "growing block universe theory" that states that we do live in a block universe, but the future hasn't happened yet. The block universe of the past continues to grow. But for cosmologists like Cortês, this still feels wrong because it means that the past exists *now* just as the present does.

I should add that one of the fundamental beliefs behind block universe theory is entropy—the seemingly natural gradual decline from order to disorder . . . whether it is your work desk going from organized to messy or an entire planet going from thriving to dying. The second law of thermodynamics says that entropy is always increasing. Basically, some scientists who disagree with the block universe theory question if the universe was much more organized just after the big bang happened—a highly rare occurrence to begin with—and just became less organized as time moved forward. Essentially, the entropy increasing from the point of the big bang is what we experience as time. But again, this is just a theory.

Theories come from our brain, our mind, which, as we talked about just a little while ago, is akin to a massive super computer. This is where we need to understand something that is, I believe, key to understanding not only scripting but also what is actually going on in the world: perception versus reality.

Seven

Selecting the Nexus, or How to Break Out of the Simulation for $0

Language is lacking in words to express new knowledge. Seemingly contradictory words must be used in the hope that the intent will be understood by taking all that is herein written and putting it together, rather than in trying to find comprehension through the analysis of a few inadequate words in isolated paragraphs.

WALTER RUSSELL, *THE UNIVERSAL ONE*

GLITCH IN THE MATRIX

One of my favorite places on the internet over the past few years is a forum on Reddit called "Glitch in the Matrix," or GITM. More recently, as I put the finishing touches on this book in late 2019, another related forum on Reddit, "Randonauts," has captured my attention, but more on that in a little while.

Reddit, for those of you who aren't familiar, is one of the world's largest online forums—with topics called "subs" (short for "subtopic"), covering everything from recipes to rock stars. You can find subs for pretty much anything from Middle Eastern recipes to fan club groups for television shows ranging from *The Golden Girls* to *The Good Place*. I initially stumbled upon the GITM forum by accident in the summer of 2018. For a few years, I had read articles online that collated and collected the best of GITM stories submitted online, but I had never really seriously explored the board on Reddit until about halfway through 2018.

Many of the accounts on this fascinating forum are the modern-day equivalent of the ghost stories that were proliferated during the Victorian era (though there are plenty of stories that may seem like ghost stories to some—more on that coming up). The board moderators make very clear, however, that it isn't a paranormal forum, and it's also not a place for creative writers to write fiction (it happens on occasion; however the moderators are excellent at both spotting fakers and enforcing the rules). This is a place where people share stories from their real lives that make no sense when we try to apply the accepted laws of nature. The name is taken from the hit movie *The Matrix,* in which a man discovers that the world around him is not what it seems but instead is an elaborate computer rendering with his actual body existing somewhere else.

Without veering too far into the world of conspiracy, the board somehow maintains a sense of reality and integrity. These are everyday people, like you and me, who have experienced things that are not normal and for which they have no explanation. If we are picturing our brains as a computer, the idea behind this online forum is that perhaps our brains are a computer inside of some sort of reality that is itself like a computer. Not every single person who participates in this forum believes this is what is going on, of course, but at the very least, most of us are sure of one thing: *something* is going on that doesn't seem to be easily explained by what we commonly understand to be the laws and nature of reality as they are currently presented to us as a whole.

The forum board instructs users to always consider "Occam's razor": the well-accepted theory that the most basic explanation for something is usually the correct one. There are also rules in place on the forum for posting stories, including the following:

- You cannot have been under the influence of drugs or alcohol when the experience took place.
- The experiences must be real with post verification if possible (photos, for example).
- The stories cannot be about experiences that took place during childhood or are from more than a few years ago; the sooner the incident happened and was reported, the better.

This is where the real-life stories on the GITM forum become the most interesting. Of course there are statistically going to be many stories that are lies or embellishments or have just been made up, but that still leaves a giant percentage of people posting stories that are true from their perspective.

I have spent thousands of hours studying the posts, and I have found a few things that fascinate me greatly. For one, the most seemingly benign stories are often the most interesting when investigated further. An example is the post titled "I know that I don't exist." While there is always a chance that the author of this post is not being truthful, his story is a prime example of what a "glitch" is—and, perhaps more importantly, what people tend to experience afterward. I encourage you to read the full post on Reddit. I've briefly outlined it here, with a couple of key quotes.

The background: One night he was preparing a bag to bring to work and to the gym the next day. He had a bunch of four bananas and ripped the bunch in half, packing two in the bag and placing the other two that he wasn't taking with him in the fridge. However, he got worried that the two bananas he had packed would spoil, so he took them out of the bag and put them in the fridge. Then he wrote himself a note that night that simply said "bananas" and put it near his fridge, so he would remember to grab his bananas out of it in the morning. The next day, he went into his kitchen and

took the bananas out and immediately and unmistakably noticed that they were again in a bunch, naturally connected. I have never before been so sure that it was an impossible error. I knew in my guts and when I ripped them again, listening to the sound of them being torn, I knew that yesterday's [account] of doing it was erased.

My mind was speeding to cross out all the possibilities and the last one was eliminated when I saw the piece of paper saying "bananas" on the table. It was not a dream. [Two] of the fruits were in my bag for a good 10 minutes and now they were again a bunch, not glued, not taped, not placed next to each other . . . I was holding a bunch. I examined the fridge, [and] there was no more fruit in the whole apartment.[1]

Though this could be written off as simply a story of someone who has not remembered correctly, what he wrote next is beyond fascinating. He describes how an overwhelming force, *which I myself have experienced exactly as he describes it,* seemed to overcome him, almost forcing him to forget the glitch. He realized that he had experienced similar glitches in the past but ignored them. He concluded:

And THAT feeling is even more convincing than the glitch itself that we do not have any idea what we are or about the world we are in. It may be a computer, a dream, I don't know. All I know for sure is that this is not real and even as I write it I feel it is of no importance. It is so not worth mentioning that I know the day after tomorrow, I will forget, I will lose interest in it. I may even detest coming back to it, to this story. It's stronger than me, but for now the image of the . . . circumstance stays with me. . . . Let this story written against all odds be a memento for something that is soon to be gone.[2]

Many other stories—hundreds per day—are posted to the GITM forum. While bananas appearing reconnected may not seem that startling, there are many people from across the globe who experience similar strangeness. With that said, the weird factor absolutely gets higher exponentially. I have sifted through thousands of these posts, and I have come up with a sampling here to show you some of the major themes that arise in many peoples' experiences.

Quantum immortality (viscerally experiencing one's own death). Examples include the post "Died on the corner," in which the author of the post describes working at a pizza place waving a sign on the corner of the street to attract business. While out on the corner one day, he sees and experiences a van jump the curb and slam into his body. He blacks out and then comes to and realizes that the accident did not occur. He goes back into the pizza place only to see the van he saw before careen into that corner.[3]

Similarly, "I literally died—or so I thought" tells of how the author of the post was commuting to work and got into a terrible car accident, with specific memories of a major head injury; she sees a light and then "wakes up" to find herself in the same place where the accident occurred, except the accident never happened.[4]

Reality slips, major and minor. One in-depth example is the post "This isn't my apartment?" A man and his girlfriend owned an apartment on the fifty-sixth floor in a secure building with the owners only having a swipe-key elevator entrance to the floor on which they live—meaning they couldn't take the elevator to other floors. The girlfriend's sister and mother were visiting for a holiday. After a quick trip to the store with his girlfriend and her sister, they swipe their card in the elevator as usual and the elevator door goes up and opens. They all notice that the usually shiny chrome numbers on the apartment doors look dusty and old. They see their apartment number and open the door, only to see a person on their couch, who says nothing. Thinking he may have done the impossible and opened the door to the wrong apartment with his key, the man closes the door. They swipe their card and go to the fifty-sixth floor "again." This time they enter their apartment, and they noticed that a bunch of things the three of them had left in the "right" apartment were all slightly moved or in the wrong place. They all distinctly remember the scent of burned toast. Their mother, who had stayed in the apartment and not come with them, looked and acted very slightly off. Then the three of them stepped onto the balcony, and smelt the exact same smell of burnt toast. We were on the balcony for all of about 30 seconds. Once we stepped back inside, everything was back where we left it, and their mother was back as we remembered her.[5]

Time slips, major and minor. An example with an emotional punch is the post "It's part of the reason we bought the house." A woman, her family, and a realtor were looking at homes in 2009. They found a house they loved, and while they were there, they all saw a black poodle in the neighbor's yard. Everyone in the family loved poodles, and they had had a family poodle who died in 2007. They decided that seeing the poodle was a good sign and ended up buying the home. A few months after moving in, when the woman mentioned the poodle to her neighbor and how her family were also "poodle people," the neighbor was confused. She told the woman that her poodle had been dead for years.[6]

Another subtle time slip example is described in the post "Cool, simple glitch?" The author of the post was sitting in her bed reading when she heard the distant sound of glass shattering. She jumped out of bed and checked her car, the kitchen, and other parts of her house to find that nothing had broken and then returned to her bedroom. A few minutes later, her daughter called to her from the kitchen saying that she needed help because she had just dropped a glass and it had shattered all over the floor. The woman asked her daughter if she had waited to call for her after the glass broke, and the daughter replied that no, she called as soon as the glass fell.[7]

Physical objects changing form and presence. An example is the post "Jewelry glitch." A woman received two pairs of earrings for her high school graduation: one was a pair of diamonds and the other a pair of sapphires. About ten years after she received the earrings, she lost one of the diamond earrings. She kept the remaining diamond with her pair of sapphire earrings in case the diamond match ever showed up. More recently, she was heartbroken when one of the sapphire earrings' clasp broke, rendering it unwearable. She kept the broken sapphire earring with its intact mate in her one-and-only jewelry box along with her single diamond earring. She then received a new pair of sapphire stud earrings as a gift. When she went to put them in her jewelry box, she was stunned to find that the broken sapphire earring was now completely and perfectly normal, and the old pair of sapphire earrings could be worn again—but the remaining diamond earring was gone.[8]

The examples go on and on, and while the contributors and commenters on the board immediately try to help rule out things like carbon monoxide poisoning, head trauma, mental illness, and dissociative identity disorder, we are still left with a staggering amount of strange stories and life experiences from people.

What I find most intriguing about GITM is that it takes many of the things we think we have an explanation for—like ghost stories and tales of aliens and/or UFOs—and puts these decidedly more grounded ideas into question. Maybe what we have been calling hauntings or fill-in-the-blank sci-fi movie plots are something else entirely—potentially because we now have the language to better describe what may be actually happening. Maybe we have never had the proper words to describe what we are experiencing when something completely out of the ordinary happens.

Some people on the forum post stories about standing in a room and suddenly seeing a person next to them or in front of them. Another theme seems to be people walking either into or out of a place that is completely abandoned and silent, when just a minute before it was full of people. There are many, many stories of people driving down roads that they later discover don't exist on any map or GPS. A sizable group of people also find themselves in some strange restaurant or gas station where it almost feels like the other people there are lifeless—still, silent, staring ahead. Or they experience the opposite (yet still unsettling) experience where they will go into a diner where everyone knows them by name.

So when you remove the liars and the people experiencing some sort of mental lapse and you factor in things like Occam's razor and Baader-Meinhof phenomenon (when someone points out something like the number 11:11, and your brain starts to notice it everywhere), we are left with one question: *What the hell is going on?!*

NO WORDS

As I found myself researching and digging deeper into this world of Glitch in the Matrix stories, I knew there was a connection to scripting. I found that people have given some pretty phenomenal suggestions for what is happening when these glitches occur. The thing that I find so enriching about these online worlds, where people from all over the globe can connect in a (mostly) positive way, is that ideas, articles, and books are recommended that most of us may never have discovered or heard of otherwise.

Once you get past the people suggesting that glitches are more proof of quantum physics, some revolutionary and groundbreaking scientific literature is suggested that might explain the reasoning behind these seemingly unexplainable things happening to everyday people like you and me.

This is where things get both exciting and extremely frustrating. Exciting because there is finally some movement toward explaining these things—scripting included—that isn't just quantum physics. Fresh, new ideas are finally bubbling to the surface. The frustrating thing is that we don't really have the language or words to properly describe them.

Even the phrase "Glitch in the Matrix" conjures up (for me, at least) notions of an alien world where we are all brains in a jar living out some alien's video-game dream. This problem of lacking the proper words to describe something incredibly new and revolutionary is *not* a new one.

As Walter Russell wrote in his book *The Universal One* (first published in 1926), "Language is lacking in words to express new knowledge. Seemingly contradictory words must be used in the hope that the intent will be understood by taking all that is herein written and putting it together, rather than in trying to find comprehension through the analysis of a few inadequate words in isolated paragraphs."[9]

One of the newest and most interesting (I'd even venture to say exciting) theories about what is happening when we experience a glitch is that we are in what is referred to as a "simulation." Now, before you think I've lost my mind, I will say that I hate the word *simulation* because I think it turns so many people off. I think that the word itself is hovering over the area of the truth, but it is not quite accurate.

But here is what is incredible: the great minds and scientists of our time from Stephen Hawking and Elon Musk to Neil deGrasse Tyson all believe that there is anywhere from a 20 to 90 percent chance we are living in a simulation. Seriously. So for that reason alone, we are going to explore it for a moment and what it could mean for scripting.

THE SIMULATION THEORY

A 2016 article from the *Guardian* was titled "Is Our World a Simulation? Why Some Scientists Say It's More Likely Than Not" and included the tag line: "A swath of technologists and physicists believe that 'simulation theory' will be proved, just as it was proved that the Earth was not the center of the universe."[10]

The simulation theory was first presented in 2003 by philosopher Nick Bostrom. It is important to note that he made this prediction before YouTube, Facebook, Twitter, social media as a whole, Oculus Rift, tablets, and smart phones were invented. He made this prediction before the average person could walk into a department store like Target or Walmart and buy a virtual reality headset.

The theory is simple, and though there is some probability theory that underlies it, the concept can be understood regardless of the math. It states that, in the very near future (some futurists believe less than thirty-five to forty years), civilization will have enough computing and programming abilities that they will be able to run what Bostrom calls "ancestor simulations."

As Bostrom put it in a 2006 paper:

> These would be detailed simulations of the simulators' predecessors—detailed enough for the simulated minds to be

conscious and have the same kinds of experiences we have. Think of an ancestor simulation as a very realistic virtual reality environment, but one where the brains inhabiting the world are themselves part of the simulation. . . .

The conclusion is that at least one of the following three propositions must be true:

1. Almost all civilisations at our level of development become extinct before becoming technologically mature.
2. The fraction of technologically mature civilisations that are interested in creating ancestor simulations is almost zero.
3. You are almost certainly living in a computer simulation.[11]

What? So how did Bostrom and his colleagues come to these rather, uh, grim conclusions? They first assume that the first conclusion is false. That would mean that a large number of civilizations at our level become technologically mature. Then they suppose that the second conclusion is also false. This would mean that a large number of these technologically mature civilizations run ancestor simulations. If both one and two are false, then that means there would be minds just like ours, only simulated.

It is important to note, I believe, that Bostrom assigns less than a 50 percent chance that we are living in a simulation.[12] He puts his own personal belief at about 20 percent, which, in my opinion, is still a fairly large percentage. It is common among the leading thinkers of our day to assign a percentage of how likely it is that we live in a simulation.

As technology has made astonishing and rapid advancements in the almost two decades since the simulation theory was first introduced, many brilliant minds have come out publicly in support of the idea that we may be in a simulation. Elon Musk has famously stated that he believes there is only a one in a billion chance that we are living in "base reality,"[13] a.k.a. the real world. A scientist who works at NASA's Jet Propulsion Lab, Rich Terrile, has plainly stated that soon, in his opinion, technology will easily allow us to replicate consciousness.[14]

Astronomer Neil deGrasse Tyson hosted a forum of scientists in

2016 where he argued that the universe is " very likely" a simulation.[15] In this forum, which is available to watch on YouTube,[16] scientists from every arena broke down the idea of simulation. While some say that it is absolutely likely, others say that it is even silly to be asking the question of whether we are in a simulation.

If someone wants to disprove or prove that we live in a simulation, they have to do it in one of two ways: (1) look for evidence (such as glitches) that we are living in a simulation or (2) find the limitation or "wall" of our simulation—kind of like Jim Carrey did in his classic film *The Truman Show*. Famed physicist René Descartes had a very good understanding of simulation in a time when the word didn't exist. He proposed the evil demon theory; it was the precursor to the famous brain-in-vat theory, which is the idea that he could be existing somewhere as a brain in a jar being fed information from some unknown intelligence.[17]

Eventually Descartes reasoned that God is fair and wouldn't allow humans to be tricked. He eventually moved past this and believed that he couldn't possibly be thinking the thoughts he was thinking and exist elsewhere. In other words, the fact that a person could think proved, to Descartes, that the person existed somewhere.[18]

As the *Guardian* article states, quoting Terrile again (and remember, this is a NASA scientist working at one of the most prestigious labs on Earth):

"Quite frankly, if we are not living in a simulation, it is an extraordinarily unlikely circumstance," [Terrile] added.

So who has created this simulation?

"Our future selves," said Terrile.[19]

Like the decades of cherry-picking pieces of quantum physics to fit their view, there is already an emerging trend for people in the spiritual/ New Thought/manifesting circles to label *everything* a simulation. This is a trend that must be stemmed, or, at the very least, slowed down until we have further evidence.

We need to be talking about this, because I think it holds the *directions* to the key to the locked door of the truth of our reality and how it really operates, but I don't believe it is the key itself. The key to understanding *why* incredible tools like scripting can have legitimate, observable impacts on our reality is closer to being discovered than many realize.

PERCEPTION < REALITY

Scripting allows us to interact with someone—ourselves—and alter the reality of our world. Ever since I discovered the correct way to script, I have been searching for what it uses to operate or how it works. As discoveries in science and technology are made, I am always fascinated to see if they can help explain how seemingly otherworldly tools like scripting operate.

Donald Hoffman, a professor and cognitive scientist from the University of California, Irvine, presented a TED talk in 2015 laying out what he and his many research students had discovered.[20] Hoffman has spent the past three decades studying perception, artificial intelligence, evolutionary game theory, and the brain, and I believe his discoveries may hold the "key to the key" that unlocks the door to understanding manifesting. In his twenty-minute talk, he takes the audience on an incredible journey that leads to one pretty astounding conclusion: *evolution does not favor reality.* Put another way: as we have evolved, our evolution has not made our perception of reality anywhere close to a priority. In fact, evidence suggests that the reality and nature of our world is something evolution (biologically speaking) saw as nonessential.

In the world of science, this is both a risky and game-changing statement. Hoffman begins his explanation by asking a simple question: If he sees a red tomato one meter away and then closes his eyes and sees a gray field, does that mean that in his reality the tomato is still there? It sounds like a silly question, but the answer is that he would *think* reality is that a tomato is only a meter away even when his eyes are closed, but could his perception of reality be wrong?

Humanity once believed that Earth was flat because that was how it looked. Copernicus and Galileo helped us to realize that we were, in fact, wrong. Hoffman reminds us that this discovery made Galileo question how else we might be misinterpreting; Galileo wrote, "I think that tastes, odors, colors, and so on reside in consciousness. Hence if the living creature were removed, all these qualities would be annihilated."

Let's take the sense of vision as an example. Vision is an incredibly complex process involving "billions of neurons and trillions of synapses."

We think of [vision] as like a camera. It just takes a picture of objective reality as it is. Now, there is a part of vision that's like a camera: the eye has a lens that focuses an image on the back of the eye where there are 130 million photoreceptors, so the eye is like a 130-megapixel camera. But that doesn't explain the billions of neurons and trillions of synapses that are engaged in vision. What are these neurons up to?

Well, neuroscientists tell us that they are creating, in real time, all the shapes, objects, colors, and motions that we see. It feels like we're just taking a snapshot of this room the way it is, but in fact, we're constructing everything that we see. We don't construct the whole world at once. We construct what we need in the moment.[21]

But what if what we think we need in the moment actually doesn't help us survive? He gives the example of the Australian jewel beetle—an animal that has lived thousands, if not millions, of years surviving in the Outback. The beetles are glossy, dimpled, and brown. The males fly around looking for females (which are flightless) to mate with. This species was successful for thousands (and possibly millions) of years, until another species—*Homo sapiens* (humans)—started throwing beer bottles into the Outback.[22]

It just so happened that these beer bottles were dimpled, glossy, and brown, and the male Australian jewel beetle population tried to mate with the beer bottles exclusively. Australia ended up having to change their beer bottles to prevent the beetle from going extinct![23]

Hoffman says, "It looked like they saw reality as it is, but apparently not. Evolution had given them a hack. A female is anything dimpled, glossy, and brown, the bigger the better. Even when crawling all over the bottle, the male couldn't discover his mistake."[24]

In this case, the hack, which was meant to ensure the beetles' evolutionary fitness and survival, actually led to the opposite. Hoffman then raises and answers an important technical question:

> Does natural selection really favor seeing reality as it is? Fortunately, we don't have to wave our hands and guess; evolution is a mathematically precise theory. We can use the equations of evolution to check this out. We can have various organisms in artificial worlds compete and see which survive and which thrive and which sensory systems are more fit.
>
> So in my lab, we have run hundreds of thousands of evolutionary game simulations with lots of different randomly chosen worlds and organisms that compete for resources in those worlds. Some of the organisms see all of the reality, others see just part of the reality, and some see none of the reality, only fitness. *Who wins?*
>
> Well, I hate to break it to you, but perception of reality goes extinct. In almost every simulation, organisms that see none of reality but are just tuned to fitness drive to extinction all the organisms that perceive reality as it is. So the bottom line is, evolution does not favor veridical, or accurate, perceptions. Those perceptions of reality go extinct.[25]

This is a stunning discovery, and the implications of what this can mean for mankind are, in many ways, more mind-blowing than much of what is happening in quantum physics—mainly because this is not theory . . . it is provable fact. But, what does it mean, exactly, that evolution does not favor accurate perception of reality? These equations show that organisms (including us) don't see the true "real reality" due to evolutionary hacks "installed" to keep us alive. "It's as hard for us to let go of space-time and objects as it is for the jewel beetle to let go of its bottle. Why? Because we're blind to our own blindnesses."[26]

This is fascinating, but with our intuition telling us this can't be so, we need some help . . . I mean, how can *not* perceiving reality as it truly is be *helpful*? We have a wonderful metaphor in our modern lives: the desktop interface of a computer or laptop; namely, an icon on your desktop that is holding the notes and speech for your upcoming TED talk.

> Now, the icon is blue and rectangular and in the lower right corner of the desktop. Does that mean that the text file itself in the computer is blue, rectangular, and in the lower right-hand corner of the computer? Of course not. Anyone who thought that misinterprets the purpose of the interface. It's not there to show you the reality of the computer.
>
> In fact, it's there to hide that reality. You don't want to know about the diodes and resistors and all the megabytes of software. If you had to deal with that, you could never write your text file or edit your photo. So the idea is that evolution has given us an interface that hides reality and guides adaptive behavior. Space and time, as you perceive them right now, are your desktop. Physical objects are simply icons in that desktop.[27]

Hoffman explains that when he gives this real-life example, people will tell him to go stand in front of a train going 200 mph to prove that reality is not what we perceive. Hoffman has a great sense of humor, and, thankfully, has no plan to stand in front of an oncoming train for the same reason he won't drag that little blue icon folder of his TED talk into the desktop interface's trash can:

> Not because I take the icon literally—the file is not literally blue or rectangular—but I do take it seriously. I could lose weeks of work. Similarly, evolution has shaped us with perceptual symbols that are designed to keep us alive. We'd better take them seriously. If you see a snake, don't pick it up. If you see a cliff, don't jump off. They're designed to keep us safe, and we should take them seriously. That does not mean that we should take them literally. That's a logical error. . . .

We're inclined to think that perception is like a window on reality as it is. The theory of evolution is telling us that this is an incorrect interpretation of our perceptions. *Instead, reality is more like a 3-D desktop that's designed to hide the complexity of the real world and guide adaptive behavior.* Space as you perceive it is your desktop. Physical objects are just the icons in that desktop. [my emphasis][28]

Now that, my friends, is one of the most compelling explanations for what is happening when we script and manifest that I have ever come across. If we think back to when we talked about our brain's reticular activating system (our ExtraCom System), we know that we train it to focus on what we tell it to focus on. Our ExtraCom goes to work doing two things:

1. Finding as many examples of the item of focus in our reality that would have otherwise been filtered (like the number 11:11).
2. Searching for and pointing out opportunities to achieve or further manifest the goal we have selected (for instance, opportunities to increase passive income in your bank account).

Though Hoffman doesn't directly make the connection, it is easy to infer that our ExtraCom System has a crucial role in how we have evolved to perceive reality. Scripting is a way to retune our ExtraCom System to suddenly see the areas of reality we aren't already hardwired to see and experience. Scripting opens up new gates and doorways to potential realities for us—it is likely that we aren't creating these future realities out of thin air. I am pretty sure there aren't even multiple realities, just multiple paths and roads in *our* reality that lie just behind the veil of what we have evolved to see.

Let's take Hoffman's explanation of reality—that there is a lot of uncharted world out there that we don't see—and think of this reality as a spinning globe with a map that you would find in a schoolroom. We then can look at scripting as a tool to program the "GPS" in our brain to take a left instead of going straight at the next green light as it moves forward in the uncharted reality. This research, and what continues to be discovered (such as what we are about to discuss), continually fills me with excitement and passion because I can feel how close we are to having the map to our desires. . . . We already have two of the three things: our brain's GPS and the understanding that there is a whole world or globe of reality that is uncharted—or is it? What appears to be missing is a map. Now, a simple tool using an incredibly complex quantum computer is generating actual maps on our cell phones leading people to some incredible new worlds . . . right within their own neighborhood!

Let's tie up Hoffman's speech before we dig a little deeper into this crazy new quantum mapping and what may or may not be possible if we utilize it correctly with scripting. Hoffman reminds us that we used to think the world was flat and Earth was the unmoving center of the universe, and we were wrong. He is open to many new and exciting possibilities such as the notion that reality is some machine creating our experience (though he doubts this, as do I). Could reality be a huge group of networking conscious beings causing each other's experiences? This is something he is currently researching.[29]

Hoffman himself and his discovery bridge the boundary between neuroscientists and quantum physicists. While neuroscientists try to understand how such a thing as first-person reality can exist, quantum physicists grapple with understanding how anything *but* a first-person reality can exist. His discoveries about reality and perception raise an interesting point. Perceptions we have gained through evolution guide our adaptive behaviors, which keep us alive. This realization is one of the closest connections between science and New Thought that has ever been publicly stated—but Hoffman is not alone.

TECHNOLOGICAL SINGULARITY . . . OR SCRIPTING?

Geordie Rose is a tech visionary and founder of D-Wave Systems, Inc., a groundbreaking quantum computing company. In 2013, Rose gave a talk at IdeaCity that went viral.[30] While describing quantum computers, he explained that he believes these machines are actually interacting with and will soon be able to communicate with parallel universes. He described how the machines have to make a sound in a perfect-zero temperature environment and that these massive black box quantum machines sound like a heartbeat when standing next to them.

His famous quote from that lecture was when he said that standing near these machines made him feel like he was standing next to the "altar to an alien god." Quantum computing is an important part of manifesting, and I truly believe it will be a large topic of discussion in New Thought in the very near future. Many people have come to refer to quantum computers as "highly advanced Ouija boards"—a joke with some interesting undertones.

Rose made quite a few astonishing statements in this now famous talk. He introduced a wider audience to a quote from one of the founders of quantum computation, David Deutsch: "Quantum computation . . . will be the first technology that allows useful tasks to be performed in collaboration with parallel universes."[31]

While his talk is fascinating and I highly recommend it, something he said that bypassed many people is what struck me as the most interesting. He said, "People from a physics background love [quantum computing]. They want to understand the world, they want to understand the universe—how it all works."[32]

Is that not the same goal of so many pioneers, teachers, students, and seekers in the world of New Thought, manifesting, positive thinking, and spirituality? I know for myself that this is the case. There lies an interesting bridge between the seeker and the scientist that currently neither seems ready to cross.

In the past two decades, futurists Vernor Vinge and Ray Kurzweil put forth the fascinating idea known as the "technological singularity" into the mainstream consciousness. Depending on your age, if you asked your parents if they ever envisioned a world where artificial intelligence abounded, a mysterious entity known as "Google" provided most of the information we sought, and wireless networks connected the world, your parents would say they absolutely did not see it coming.

An article on Futurism explains it this way:

> History is full of cases in which a new and groundbreaking technology, or a collection of such technologies, completely changes people's lives. The change is often so dramatic that people who've lived before the technological leap have a very hard time understanding how the subsequent generations think. To the people before the change, the new generation may as well be aliens in their way of thinking and seeing the world.
>
> These kinds of dramatic shifts in thinking are called *Singularity*—a phrase that is originally derived from mathematics and describes a point which we are incapable of deciphering its exact properties. It's that place where the equations basically go nuts and make no sense any longer.[33]

Kurzweil, one of the futurists I mentioned above, is now the director of engineering at Google. One of the most fascinating things about Kurzweil is that he has had a seemingly uncanny ability to predict the future of technology. His track record spans more than two decades, and he has predicted everything from handheld smart phones to social networks to scientific breakthroughs in medicine and all worlds of science (many of these predictions were made in the 1990s!). He is both feared and loved by many for his ability to use his knowledge of technological advancements to predict where we are headed.

I cannot stress enough just how amazing his track record has been. This is why many are afraid of his biggest prediction—what most of his predictions since the 1990s have been leading up to—which is that, by 2045, humanity will reach the singularity by creating a superhuman artificial intelligence (AI). He believes that this AI will invent and create things that we cannot even conceive of and that it will be intelligent enough to improve itself and make itself smarter and better. Then the next generation would do the same: improve itself and make itself even smarter. This would lead to an explosion of intelligence beyond anything we could ever imagine, leaving our poor, lesser biological minds to wonder in awe at what we have created.

I want to make the distinction between the technological singularity and the other singularity often described in New Age circles as the ultimate realization that all beings are one and has humanity ending in some "Kumbaya" hippie fever dream. I believe that we are all connected, but not all one. I want to make clear that I do not believe that humans are heading for a spiritual moment where we all coagulate into one being.

Kurzweil has been wrong before, but his track record lies somewhere around 70 to 80 percent accuracy, and it all leads to the idea of the singularity. He has predicted that in the twenty-first century, this superhuman AI will eventually want rights and to be recognized as being conscious. The notion of any type of technological singularity has scared many great minds. Elon Musk and the late Stephen Hawking both expressed concern.

While some are afraid of this, others see that maybe a singularity does not automatically equate to a robot revolution. Garry Kasparov, who was the first professional chess player to be beaten by an AI named Deep Blue, did not despair after his defeat. Instead he went on to create new kinds of chess competitions in which AI and the player collaborated. In these incredible collaborations, the computer suggests the best possible moves for the player, and the player must decide which move is the best. These collaborations have allowed the humans and AI to have more and better success than either would have had on their own.

Kurzweil does not believe that the coming singularity is anything to fear. "Ultimately, it will affect everything. We're going to be able to meet the physical needs of all humans. We're going to expand our minds and exemplify these artistic qualities that we value."[34] He firmly believes that the science-fiction version of AI enslaving us is silly—it is there to improve us.

"What's actually happening is [machines] are powering all of us," Kurzweil said.

They're making us smarter. They may not yet be inside our bodies, but, by the 2030s we will connect our neocortex, the part of our brain where we do our thinking, to the cloud. We're going to get more neocortex, we're going to be funnier, we're going to be better at music, we're going to be sexier.... We're really going to exemplify all the things that we value in humans to a greater degree.[35]

"That's great," you may say. "The guy from Google, the world's foremost technology company, is telling us not to be afraid of its creations—what a joke! This is all about them making money, humanity be damned!" But, I happen to agree with Kurzweil—I don't think what is coming is scary at all. I firmly believe that, as technology and science grow and advance, so does the world of New Thought. I believe that the two worlds are on a path to merging, which will lead to greater understanding.

Technology, science, and spiritual understanding are much more connected than many in either field would care to admit. Just look at history; it's full of examples. One of the most seemingly unlikely places for this kind of discussion online, the technological and scientific Singularity Weblog, posted a fascinating article in 2010 that discussed the connection between spirituality and technology. In the article, Matt Swayne wrote:

Over the eons, our conception of God has formed and reformed into the shape of our technology. . . . Early man saw gods and goddesses as hunters or warriors. . . . As the Renaissance approached, God was . . . a clockmaker, an expert, deterministic mathematician that only a Newtonian physicist could worship. As the twentieth century dawned . . . God became not just a computer scientist, but a quantum computer scientist.[36]

He adds something that I consider to be not only profound but also encouraging coming from a website entrenched in the world of science:

Looking ahead, as greater and greater technological power appears on our horizon, we can speculate how this rapid change will influence our philosophies. . . . Or, perhaps, the Singularity must wait on us. It must wait for our imagination to adapt to these new possibilities before change is even possible.

The Singularity, then, will ultimately become less about machines. And more about spirit [emphasis mine].[37]

So, with all we have learned, we must narrow the field of possibility to find what is actually happening when we script. Are we just constantly jumping from dimension/parallel universe to parallel universe? Perhaps all of those dimensions ARE already boxed in as one in a block time, and our free will is choosing which of the infinite line of possible dimensions we want to walk into.

THE FATUM BOT

The Fatum Bot is a free tool that, after months of personally trying it out with Solly, I now believe is the first step to using technology to bring your manifestations into reality. At the very least, this tool has shown me that we are headed into an era where technology shows us the map to new physical realities, which in my experience can be used to manifest what we want in conjunction with scripting. If you have internet access and a smart phone, you have access to this incredible tool, which is connected to a real quantum computer located at the Center for Computation and Communication Technology located at Australian National University. It is part of a project called the Fatum Project.

I found out about the Fatum Project and the Fatum Bot through someone on—where else?—the Glitch in the Matrix forum on Reddit. It was spring of 2019, and when I first read about this then fledgling project, I knew this tied into everything I've spent my life studying. Per the official forum:

The Fatum Project was born as an attempt to research unknown spaces outside predetermined probability-tunnels of the holistic world and has become a fully functional reality-tunnel creating machine that digs rabbit holes to wonderland. We are utilizing the fatum project's quantum random location generator telegram bot to generate random coordinates to travel the multiverse.[38]

What? I know. That description may sound like a mouthful (and a mind-full!), and I was a little apprehensive the first time I read that explanation. Thankfully, after months of experimenting and studying my own participation with the project, I can now explain it in simpler terms (with the help of the wonderful resource guide). Let's start with something that is, to me (and hundreds of thousands of mathematicians, scientists, and everyday people around the globe), one of the creepiest, weirdest things ever: The Sierpinski Triangle.

Fig. 6.4. The Sierpinski Triangle
(image by Beojan Stanislaus, CC-by-sa 3.0)

While this may seem to the average person like a pretty drawing of triangles layered over each other, it is much, much more than that. Feel free to go to my website, RoyceChristyn.com, where I will have a video of the triangle being created in real time using a pair of dice and a marker.[39] For those of you who don't want to watch the video yet, know that it shows something called the "chaos game": a math game in which one takes a marker, paper, and set of dice and makes three points on the paper to indicate the points on a triangle. The person then labels the points A, B, and C and makes a single mark or dot anywhere on the paper. The rules are simple: if you roll a 1 or 2, you make a dot halfway between your most recently drawn dot and point A; if you roll a 3 or 4, you mark the next dot halfway between your most recent dot and point B; and if you roll a 5 or 6, you make the mark halfway between your last mark and point C. There are tons of free versions of this game online where you can set your points and have a computer roll the dice for you (this makes for quick visual results), or you can do it the old-fashioned way. No matter which way you choose to experiment with the chaos game, you absolutely will create the Sierpinski Triangle, blank spaces and all. The game has evolved with computers, and even creepier discoveries have been made when the person shifts the amount of points on the blank sheet, such as reproducing perfect three-dimensional images of ferns and other natural creations.[40]

I highly recommend watching the video mentioned above all the way through to let the full creepiness of this settle into your mind. Not because I want you to feel creeped out, but because it is one of the very best examples that one can be shown to prove that there is something seriously up with our reality. You're probably thinking, "Royce, why am I reading about math games and triangles? What does this have to do with scripting, manifesting, and creating your reality?" Don't worry, this is me, and there is always a method to the magic . . . and that is where the Fatum Project comes into play.

See those white spaces, the blank space that makes up the white triangles? I want you to think about the overall white paper the triangle composed of blue dots sits on as a total picture or map of your own personal reality (including your home, the neighborhoods and stores you frequent, and the things you do day to day). Okay, now I want you to pretend that you are a blue marker, and every time you engage with your personal reality (which includes all of reality overall, not just yours), you make a blue mark on the white paper. No matter what you do, where you go, even (and especially) if you *think* you are being spontaneous by taking a right down a road you have never driven down on your way to the grocery store, for example, it is mathematically proven that you will never travel to the areas of the map that are in white. EVER. You can make 100 choices or 1 billion choices in your life as a blue marker, and, thanks to hundreds of years of research, science tells us that we will never make a blue dot in those blank spaces. Thinking of the overall white sheet of paper as a total map of your physical reality, including all of the buildings, natural structures, and so on around you . . . you will only ever interact with and see the buildings, people, and things located in the areas in which you make a blue dot on that sheet.

Remember when Hoffman said that when it comes to our true reality we are "blind to our blindness"? Keeping that in mind along with the triangle above, the Fatum Project's theory page has this to say about what it calls "probability blind spots":

All things in the world are causally connected with each other and everything that happens, including our thoughts, are usually determined by the sum of all environmental factors. This makes the world close to deterministic. The patterns arising in the network of these relations reduce even random actions to a limited set of possible outcomes.

This means that no matter what choices you make, and no matter how many variations on how your day may pass, there are always some places where you simply cannot be, because none of the chains of your decisions leads there.

Interesting that such places may be somewhere nearby. On your street there may be a lane in which you will never think to look and you do not even know about its existence. What could be hiding in such blind spots? And what could be hiding in places where no one looks at all? This is the first question of our experiment. There may be magical creatures or aliens or a pile of garbage, no one knows for sure.[41]

The creators of the project initially asked what the long-term effects would be of someone being in a place they never should have been. Does this cause a sort of butterfly effect, where your entire reality is shifted because you are entering what they refer to as a new "reality tunnel"? As they explain, "Even just a very different person from us can live in a completely different world, because [that person] goes on completely different routes and receives other information."[42]

The problem for years was that, to get to truly random points, you could not use a normal random number generator. You needed something that could effectively reach into other worlds and pull out locations for you to visit, eliminating all possibilities of you accidentally visiting a place that is predetermined on your end. Enter quantum computers, which have become much more accessible over the past few years. The creators of the project found two sources to combat this tricky situation. Their goal was to break our determinism completely, and the only known way to do that was to move into where the principle of uncertainty exists, using measurements from quantum computers.

SCRIPTING AWAY THE STASIS FIELD

As I've mentioned, one of the core things I have always intended was to be a master manifester. I think that has served me well, as I often find new and wonderful ways to bring things I desire into my reality. When I read about the Fatum Project, I became obsessed with the possibilities of combining the quantum tool with my scripting and manifestation work. The creators of the project made the steps to breaking out of our determined state using quantum computers extremely easy. Using a free text message app on your phone called Telegram (which is available in all app stores) you connect with the "Fatum Bot," a.k.a. the quantum computer. The whole process takes about ten minutes to set up and one minute to use whenever you want to play around with it. As of publication, the people behind the Fatum Bot are working on an app that will also be available in all app stores.

Using a private, secure server using your phone's built-in GPS, you send the Fatum Bot your location and ask it to send you the coordinates of a quantum-computer generated "attractor point" for you to travel to. You tell the app how far to look for points (I recommend between 1,000 and 5,000 meters, depending on how much walking or driving you want to do!). Within a few minutes, the app sends you back a point on a map with a "strength" number, indicating how random and out of your zone this location would be. While you can get a strength number all the way up to 9,000, anything over a strength of 2 is enough to start seeing some awesome changes in your world. Solly and I have averaged anywhere between a 1 and a 9.5—and I could write an entire book on just the experiences we have had in only a few months.

One thing that initially caught my eye about this project as it relates to manifesting was this piece of information from the FAQ:

> Although the creation of new reality-tunnels is of a purely causal-perceptual nature (you do not literally enter another world, you just have the opportunity to see and interact with new parts of it), there is also a hypothesis that an experiment may cause cases of the so-called Dimension Jumping.
>
> Many researchers have reported about changes in various details in their environment. In some cases, new buildings appeared, unusual types of merry-go-rounds on children's playgrounds, which the researcher had not seen before, but according to official data, they have existed there for several years.[43]

Solly, my mother, and I read hundreds of experiences posted on Reddit by everyday people who were having some awesome things happen when they would use the bot. Experiences are broad. They range from being led directly to murals of pictures and images that address issues and events eerily accurate as they pertain to the person (what the Fatum team now call "picture walls" that seem to "talk" to the person exploring); to leading a man who was in need of a new mattress to a house in his neighborhood he had never seen before where the owner was selling the perfect mattress; to a woman being given a point on her first try that sent her directly to a house she had just toured a week earlier on her search for a new home.

Those are mild compared to some people's experiences, like a woman who was led to a house in her neighborhood she never knew existed, but decided to knock on the door, and a childhood friend she hadn't seen in years opened the door! I suggest that you go to the Reddit website and read the "Randonauts" sub to see all of the amazing experiences recorded by people.

Solly and I decided to try it out the first day using a relatively simple strategy: we both privately wrote down words and objects on our phones' notepads and didn't tell each other what we had written. We decided to visit multiple points on our first walk—meaning we would use the bot to generate a point on the map, then once we got there we would generate a new point and walk there, and so on. One of the things the research project recommends is to pick up any trash or litter in the area the bot sends you to: they theorize that the more we interact with the environment we are sent to, the more it "crystallizes" and "forms" our new reality. Plus, if anyone sees you picking up trash or debris, you are only helping the environment!

Since we were going together, we decided that we would alternate who asked for the attractor point on the map. Solly went first, and, to his shock, we were led to the side of a street where there were hundreds of tiny shells, many perfectly "sliced" in half. His jaw dropped, as the first item he wrote in his notebook was "Fibonacci and Golden Ratio," which is the mathematical equation (or variation of) found in nature in pinecones, leaves . . . and seashells. (It's not a perfect golden ratio, but the spiral seashell/golden ratio image is one of the most commonly known.)

Excited, I typed in a new point and got directions to our next

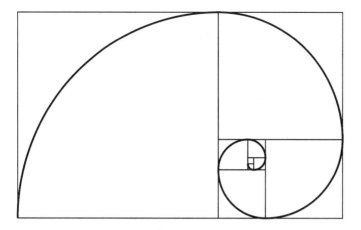

Fig. 6.5. A Fibonacci spiral

Fig. 6.6. Seashells showing the spiral shape

place. One of the things they tell you to do on your walk is to keep your eyes open for signs, objects, and so on as you walk (you *can* drive, it is just a little bit harder to take in all the weirdness, in my experience). On our way to the next point, we saw a giant plastic four-foot-long green arrow randomly lying in the middle of the street pointing in the direction we were walking, a sidewalk chalk drawing of a rainbow, the word *fake* with a drawing of a cactus, and tons of other weird "out of place" things.

We noticed immediately this amazing, indescribably tingly and sweet sensation that seems to come over us when we are going on these "quantum quests"—like a warm blanket on a cold day. It reminds me of the feeling I get when I go hiking in Sedona or near the beach to connect with nature. That feeling of being in sync with the nature around you, only this time it is in the middle of one of the biggest cities in the world! I was already excited about the chalk drawings, but I was stunned when we got to my attractor point, where there was a very large topiary (which is not common in my neighborhood, I might add) of . . . a cactus! Here is what I drew in my notes, and a photo of the sidewalk, the topiary, and the wagon wheels, which we also saw on that walk.

Fig. 6.7. Royce's note, which says "cactus," "LGBT Pride" (the symbol of which is a rainbow), and has a drawing of a wagon wheel.

We went on a few more walks using this basic method of writing down symbols or images, and I could write an entire novel on all of the meaningful things that happened. We would go to attractor points without drawing anything ahead of time and had similarly profound experiences. Some experiences felt stronger than others, and some even seemed totally normal at the time, but later we would find that just

Fig. 6.8. Rainbow chalk drawings

*Fig. 6.9. Cactus
topiary*

Fig. 6.10. Wagon wheels

the act of going on the walk changed our reality. (Such as the time the walk was a last-minute decision, because originally we had planned on not being home that day. When we got home from the walk, we ended up getting a knock on our door from a neighbor we never knew we had and are now good friends with him.)

We decided to begin incorporating more sophisticated scripting into our Fatum Bot experiments. Since we already both script daily, we decided to do an extra script on days we knew we would walk, which was only about a paragraph or two long. We do NOT write about the walk itself but rather focus intently on a certain desire or intention in our lives. The *moment* we finish our script (and make sure we are really in the feeling place of our little script), we pick up our phones and the text app to get a location. We get up, grab a bag for trash or items to collect at our point, and go out the door to the location the quantum computer has given us! We have noticed something pretty incredible: though we still see some interesting things on the walk, and sometimes we don't notice much of anything, *the short walk itself seems to pack as much punch and have as much of an effect in our world in the following days as the long Ten-Day Script*! This is pretty incredible, considering it is only a small paragraph or two versus a long script.

I have always seen our Ten-Day Script as a sort of "vitamin shot" or boost to our Daily Script manifesting, and the Fatum Bot seems to give us the same boost, with our intentions and wishes from our normal Daily Script coming into fruition fast. I always say that Tuesday is my favorite day because I usually see so many results and manifestations from my Ten-Day Script begin to materialize. Now, when I use the quantum bot, I feel like every day is Tuesday!

People often ask the moderators of the Fatum Project forum, as noted in the FAQ, "Wasn't my choice to use the project predetermined? Aren't the points I visited determined by my choice to participate in the project?" And their response is so perfect, it is best to just quote them directly:

It is predetermined, the only thing that is nondeterministic is the random location. **In theory, your fate can predetermine the participation in the project, but not visiting those exact places.**[44]

It should go without saying, but, if you want to try this out for yourself, you MUST follow the law (don't trespass, loiter, etc.), don't do anything or go anywhere you feel is unsafe, and make sure you read *everything* on the Fatum forum. You do not need to have a free Reddit account to read and research any of this.

There is a lot we don't yet know about not only the Fatum Project but also quantum computing in general. What I appreciate so much about this particular project is that, even if it were to turn out to be some giant scam (it isn't!), it still points out how predetermined the average person's life is: even if you are going to be spontaneous by going to a grocery store by taking a road you've never traveled, chances are *that* is actually predetermined. I believe that scripting will one day perhaps be thought of as the grandmother technique to the more sophisticated methods of creation that are coming in the next few decades thanks to the incredible potential that quantum computing provides. (Hello to those of you reading this one hundred years from now—I hope that you too can get something out of this little book!)

SELECTION VERSUS MANIFESTATION

Mitch Horowitz writes in his book *The Miracle Club* that he believes the key may lie in time and how we perceive it as linear. When we manifest, Horowitz writes:

> What is really happening is that we select—not manifest, but select—
> from an infinite variety of things that are occurring all at once, all
> around us. When our illusion of order is pierced by an emotive,
> focused thought, we experience what might be called a "time col-
> lapse," in which events, perceptions, and notions of past, present, and
> future all blend together. We then see the world as it really is—whole
> and not subdivided into points on an imaginary line, extending from
> birth to death.[45]

I think that Horowitz is absolutely on to something here, and it is very important. The idea of selection versus manifestation is something that I have thought about before, and I would like to take it a step further here. If it's all a simulation like a computer, then scripting and/or manifesting is as easy to explain to ourselves as it is to explain to someone that, for a computer to do anything for us, we must give it commands (like we would give the quantum Fatum Project Bot a command to retrieve a location). This also lines up with what Hoffman described as our perception of reality being the interface of something like the desktop of a computer. Intention and emotion all fuel something, but I think it's easier than that. We can give a computer commands while feeling anything from anger to elation to boredom. As long as we know how to execute the commands (and what commands to execute), the computer doesn't care what state of feeling we are in.

I have noticed in my own work that, despite the repeated warnings from well-meaning teachers, the action of just doing the work (whether that be a Daily Want List or a script) is *always* going to be more effective than not doing it at all. Of course emotion and intention are important, and I know that they have an impact on aspects of creating reality, but if I'm bored or don't feel like it, I still do them. When I don't do them, and start missing days, I can see the results in my daily life.

Many authors, speakers, and teachers say that this is a bad thing and that we should always feel "jazzed," "excited," and full of positive energy when we do our manifesting work. But I'm a human being, not a robot (yet), and I experience human emotions, including boredom. Yes, we create by a combination of feelings, thoughts, and attention/focus, but I think the all-around hack to this is that we must *intend to be a master manifester* and make that intention a cornerstone of our Daily Want List.

That has been my intention for more than fifteen years, and I have put most of my emotions and feelings into it, which has brought into my life keys like the knowledge of scripting properly and other master tools of creation. Once I have the tool, I don't need to keep flowing intense emotion and feeling toward it; I already have it and use it every single day. I believe this is important: once you have the hammer, you don't need to visualize and imagine having the hammer every time you are about to use it! Just go to your drawer or toolbox, pull out the hammer, and start pounding nails.

Watering your garden mindlessly still hydrates the plants as well as watering them with intention and thought and care. The plants still remain alive and thrive. I may be wrong, but I'd rather put forth an idea and have it be proved wrong than not put one forth at all. I think if we are selecting possible futures, it is because we are commanding them into our space like we tell a computer what website we want to visit or what words we want it to produce on our screen when we type.

If life is some sort of game, then knowing the tools of New Thought is like having the instruction manual or cheat codes to a video game. Maybe the books on New Thought can be thought of as the "[Fill in the blank] for Dummies" series of books (I say this lovingly; those Dummies books have helped millions). They hold the most basic and necessary instructions for not just playing the game but also winning our own personal levels.

I think it is more likely than not that we are operating in some sort of "real reality" that we don't have the words to describe, so the closest we can get is to call it a shifting hologram. Many aren't aware that in Stephen Hawking's final theory (released posthumously in May of 2018), he asserted that he finally believed we are living in a holographic universe.[46] Hawking had never liked the idea of a multiverse—infinite universes all with their own laws of physics. The fact that the theory of the multiverse couldn't coexist with Einstein's theory of general relativity bothered him greatly.[47]

In his final work, Hawking and his colleague and collaborator Thomas Hertog assert that the universe *expressing itself as 3-D is an illusion*. Instead they claim that we are actually experiencing a *projection* from information stored on a 2-D surface. This is pretty stunning information. Before his death, Hawking talked of these (at the time not released) findings, saying, "We are not down to a single, unique universe, but our findings imply a significant reduction of the multiverse, to a much smaller range of possible universes."[48] This lines up with

Horowitz's idea that we are selecting from a field of possible universes rather than manifesting.

I would add to this that Hawking's thought that there aren't infinite universes, just many, could help explain why sometimes we experience trouble with manifesting: Is it possible that not every conceivable future is available to us at each moment? I would venture to guess that the truth is that both ideas fit here: perhaps Hawking is correct, but the idea of having a giant number of universes overall to select from is also true.

I don't think that the quantity of potential universes/dimensions we select from and move into is infinite *at all times* (remember how predetermined our lives generally are!). With the base tools we have, we can select from a group of universes that are available to us in the moment we are making the selection/manifestation, and the *specific* universes/dimensions we get to choose from at *that moment we are choosing* are made available *based on our current state*—physically, emotionally, and mentally. I would think that it is perfectly reasonable to assume that a different set of available futures are there for us depending on where we currently are in the moment we are making the selection. (I believe that the Fatum Bot, and the many similar quantum computer tools we will all soon have access to, may help us overcome this barrier of having a selection of universes based only on our emotive states, but only time will tell.)

Another breakthrough in science went mostly unnoticed except for a few reports here and there. *Wired*'s headline sums up this profound discovery: "Cosmic Rays Offer Clue Our Universe Could Be a Computer Simulation." Scientist Silas Beane and his associates at the University of Bonn calculated that, if we are in a simulation, then we would expect there to be a sort of lattice at the edges of the universe that we can observe. Again, this is like the example of Jim Carrey's character in *The Truman Show* hitting the wall of the world the TV studio created for him.

As cosmic ray particles fly through the universe, they change direction and spread out, but as the article states, "there's a known limit to how much energy those particles have . . . and Beane and his colleagues have calculated that this seemingly arbitrary cliff in the spectrum is consistent with the kind of boundary that you'd find if there was an underlying lattice governing the limits of a simulator."[49]

There is still more work to be done in this field, but it, once again, leads us to believe there is something happening here that we do not have the words to properly define or explain. I think that if it's a simulation, then Professor Hoffman's brilliant discoveries regarding perception tell us that it's a simulation that exists inside of us, rather than us existing inside of the simulation. This is an important key. I would like to propose a new word that encompasses the essence of what we are seeing and trying to explain when we say "simulation" and, even, "hologram." I call it the *Nexus*.

NEXUS: A NEW WAY TO DESCRIBE THE "SIMULATION"

I chose the name Nexus because not only does the definition of *nexus* describe more accurately what we are experiencing with what is called the "simulation," but the name is also a way to honor a religious god known as Exu (pronounced "ex-oo," or sometimes "eh-shoo") throughout the world (more about him below). Thus the name "Nexus" itself honors the merging of science and spirituality . . . the bridging of which will actively be happening in the very near future.

Nexus is defined in the Oxford dictionary as "a connection or series of connections linking two or more things" and "the central and most important point or place." I love that the word *nexus* contains the name Exu. Why is this important to me? I first learned of Exu when I lived in New Orleans in my very early twenties. I was honored to have a chance to study the unique spiritual aspects and belief systems that are unique to the Gulf of Mexico region.

Exu is a god of many Afro-Caribbean religions stretching from Africa to South America to the Caribbean and the Gulf Coast regions of the United States. He is adored as the god of the crossroads, but he is so much more than that. "Transformations of Esu" by Kristen Hileman explains Exu this way (referring to him as *Esu,* one of a few common spellings of the name):

> Esu's power lies primarily in his unfixed and fluid nature. He is a god chiefly associated with trickery, ambivalence, communication and the crossroads, a fateful symbolic site where one's journey might take any direction. The god penetrating barriers and linking one world with the next.
>
> Esu, situated at the middle of the crossroads, is the union, bridge and threshold to the differing realms of gods and humans, as well as the intersection of chance and fate, unpredictability and order. Another physical attribute, the god's limp, is evidence of Esu's striding different worlds. The Yoruba believe that Esu walks with a limp because he has one foot in the world of the gods and the other in the world of humans.[50]

What better way to describe what everyone from Stephen Hawking to quantum computer pioneers to neuroscientists strain to describe! Like the simulation so many great minds talk about, Exu is unfixed and fluid, and yet he himself is the embodiment of trickery. What is a hologram or brilliantly executed simulation as we know it but an elaborate trick? A Nexus is where we bridge two worlds—which is another way to look at our world if it is indeed some sort of simulation, whether projected inward to the outer world or the other way around!

When Stephen Hawking and others talk about multiworlds and quantum computers being able to access parallel universes, Exu is, again, a perfect fit: he has one foot in our world and the other in the world of the unfathomable. What are we all trying to explain but something that is unfathomable? It is not hard to speculate that the inclusion of the name Exu in the word *Nexus* is not a coincidence, for it conveys that the Nexus is more than just science or spirit—it is the most important point and the connection that links both. The Nexus is an incredible term, then, to better explain this new and incredible world we are discovering.

. . .

I understand that many who study New Thought may have an aversion to all of this talk of science and technology, but the plain and simple fact is that this is where we as a civilization are headed, like it or not. I think it is a good thing. Something to be embraced and worked with.

We need to be aggressively and actively adding new thoughts, ideas, and resources to New Thought! We can't keep publishing new books that only rehash the old ideas. It's not that the principles found in New Thought don't work—quite the opposite! But they don't contain all of the ingredients to make the recipe come out perfectly, so to speak. Also, those of us who teach and study these principles shoot ourselves in the foot when we don't include details (that aren't cherry-picked) of what science could help us understand better.

The time is now. More writers and teachers are finally adding to the discussion. This wouldn't have been possible if the old New Thought teachings hadn't finally reached the masses like they did at the beginning of the twenty-first century. In recent years spiritual and New Thought studies for millions of people have erupted and reached populations they never could have before.

One of the things about the film *The Secret* that most interested me when it first came out wasn't the material itself but *how* the material was spread. Many don't know this, but I was there and saw it firsthand: Years before Netflix, the team behind *The Secret* made the film available to stream on our laptops and computers for a small fee. This led to many more sales of the physical DVD, but that isn't what is important to me. What's important is that literally millions more people were able, for the first time, to have access to these ancient teachings, which pushed them to go further to explore. This was all made possible because of breakthroughs in technology and science. People who study New Thought and spiritual studies need not see technology and science as some beast to fear. We are not going to end the world, and I don't believe the world will end with the coming technology and scientific understandings.

It will instead be, for many, the beginning. Some will disagree with me as they read this on their computers or in physical form in a book printed with technology that uses scientific breakthroughs in printing and book binding. Maybe the truth of how this all works has been something we collectively have been scripting for a very long time—and it's finally manifesting into form.

Eight

Putting It All Together

You have brains in your head. You have feet in your shoes.
You can steer yourself any direction you choose. You're on
your own. *And you know what you know. And YOU are*
the one who'll decide where to go.

DR. SEUSS, *OH, THE PLACES YOU'LL GO!*

SO, WHERE ARE WE? Though it may seem like a lot to take in, the beautiful thing is that with scripting we can see firsthand how to interact with and access this incredible new reality—the Nexus. You are not adding much to your daily routine, but a little goes a long way. To recap, when it comes down to implementing the most basic principles of scripting, you are adding four small tasks to your day:

1. Daily Want List (in the morning)
2. Daily Belief List (in the morning)
3. Daily Script (Monday through Saturday mornings)/Ten-Day Script (Sunday, any time)
4. Nightly Journal (just before bed)

Now, just so we are clear: the Ten-Day Script replaces your Daily Script on *Sundays only.* Why Sunday? Well, technically, you can choose any day of the week that works best for you. But keep in mind that after years of teaching this method to friends and family, Sunday seems to always be the day that most people can squeeze in the extra time required for the Ten-Day Script. It is also a great day for a reset or adjustment, since Sunday is the first day of every new week.

Sunday is also a good day to reflect on the previous Ten-Day Script and the daily scripting you've done all week. Whether things need to be shifted or are going perfectly, it's a great day to focus on that and implement it into your Ten-Day Script.

You will still do your Daily Want List and Belief List in the morning as always and then go about your day as usual. I often do my Ten-Day Script before bed, just before my Nightly Journal. But, truthfully, you can do your Ten-Day Script at any point during the day you have chosen as your Ten-Day Script day (in most cases, Sunday). You can even do it right after your Want List and Belief List.

Some people don't like the idea of doing these things every day, and I know that it sounds like a chore at first. I really, really do know. But I encourage you to stick with it no matter what. If you do happen to stop or forget, look at your life on the days that you don't do these relatively small, easy exercises that require only a minimal amount of time to complete. As everyone who incorporates scripting into their life finds, their life on the days that they don't script is much less satisfying than on the days that they do script. If you don't believe me, try doing the daily routine for about a month, then stop for a week—you will see exactly what I mean.

Now I want to use the rest of this chapter to address some very commonly asked questions, as well as give you some insider exercises that you can use to stretch your scripting and bring it to new levels!

FREQUENTLY ASKED QUESTIONS

Here are answers to some of the most basic questions that you may have. Note: If you don't have them yet, you will soon.

Question: What about adding/including/writing about other people in my script?

Answer: Here's the thing: I include other people in my script. Some people may consider this unethical, but I am going to explain why I think it is not only important but also often necessary to include others in your script. First of all, you have to remember that people are subconsciously scripting you into their lives each and every day—whether they are thinking about you, writing about you, or talking to others (or even you) about you. We humans are always scripting each other into the fabric of our vibrations. Does that always make an impact? Well . . . yes and no.

The best way to look at the question of writing about other people in your script is to view it from the perspective of how you write your Nightly Journal. When you do your "real" journaling at night, you talk about others and the encounters that you had with them during your day. Even if you are just keeping a normal diary or journal, you know it is perfectly normal to include other people in your recounting of the day.

This is the way you should go about including others into your scripting exercises. You don't want to write something that is negative or that would cause harm. Remember, quite literally, scripting is all about perspective: specifically YOUR perspective. Like your Nightly Journal, you want it to be about you, from your perspective.

One thing you will hear quite a bit in the world of New Thought/ positive thinking/Law of Attraction is that you can't create in another person's reality. While that isn't entirely true, as proved by my long-time study of memes and memetics, you have to keep in mind that scripting is about changing YOUR life, not someone else's! Now, I feel like a little bit of a hypocrite here, but let me give you the oldest, most common perspective on creating in another's reality (which is what some fear when they begin manifesting deliberately). I will use a passage from *Excuse Me, Your Life Is Waiting* as an example.

Grabhorn writes about what we most often do when someone is sick or in a bad way and we want to help (spoiler: we end up focusing on the other person's problem and therefore end up matching up with that vibration/frequency, which is no good). Though she is talking about what to do when we want to help someone who is sick, has lost their house, or is going through a rough time, the lesson about creating in someone else's experience is a pretty solid example of the most common line given when teachers explain our ability to create in another's experience.

Grabhorn recounts the story of her friend who had a father dying of an empty life three thousand miles away on the other side of the country. Every evening she would think she was sending her father healing thoughts, wishing for him to be happier, while only focusing on his lack—lack of friends, of a life worth living, and so on. So once this friend got wind of the Law of Attraction, she started to see her dad as he used to be: full of vitality, life, and passion. And within a few days this friend's dad called saying that he felt better than he had in years and that he wanted to fly out for a visit.

Grabhorn writes: "Was she responsible for this change? Only in providing her dad with an opportunity to pick up these new paints and brushes. She had given him a vibrational leg up, much like we might toss a life jacket to someone. They can grab it or not, but the choice is theirs, and theirs alone."[1]

I do like Grabhorn's analogy of "paints and brushes"; in short, she says that we can't paint on another's canvas, but we can offer the paints and brushes to inspire them to do so on their own. For a lot of people this explanation works and is enough. But we know now that humans are using memetics to constantly place mind viruses—whose sole purpose is to survive and replicate—into each other's heads at an almost unfathomable rate. Many of the meme "viruses" end up dictating our behavior on a level not conscious to us.

Memes, as described by Richard Brodie in his brilliant book *Virus of the Mind,* "can and do run your life, probably to a far greater degree than you realize." He goes on to explain that "the memes you are programmed with, even without considering the culture around you, affect your life in almost every conceivable way. That's why a virus of the mind is something to be taken seriously. These viruses fill your mind up with memes—ideas, attitudes, and beliefs—that make the results you get in life very different from the results you may want."[2]

Now, I don't include that here to scare you, and I will go into this more in later on, but I realize that people are constantly using tactics to create in our lives all of the time. Most of the time these people are strangers—advertising executives, anonymous people online, faceless government officials, publicists—who are implanting these memes into our lives. This is not a conspiracy fallacy; this is a real, scientifically backed fact. The great news is that scripting overrides much of this, and it allows you a way out.

So the answer for the many people who ask me, "Am I going to hurt someone by doing this?" is no. Scripting, at its core, is a purely personal action. You affect the world—and therefore the people—around you. So include others in a way that makes sense with how you would write about them in your journal. Here are two examples of how to include others in your script.

Wow! Today was a wonderful day. I was so pleased . . . when I got home from work, there was no mess anywhere! The family had gotten together and cleaned the whole house. It was awesome! Right after I got home, I got the phone call I had been waiting for, and I found out that I got the weekend job working at the theater! I am so elated and excited that I'm going to get to work with all of those talented people. I really am just beyond thrilled right now. Everyone seems to be in really great moods, and I am, too!

Wow! Today was a wonderful day. I was so pleased . . . when I got home from work, there was no mess anywhere! Little Timmy cleaned the whole house without me asking him. It was awesome! Right after I got home, Terry called me—I got the weekend job working at the theater! I am so elated and excited that I'm going to get to work with all of those talented people. I really am just beyond thrilled right now. Jon, Mary, and Bob are all in really great moods, which is making me feel excellent.

Can you spot which example is better? The one on the left still includes everything that you would like to happen, while being more general. When in doubt, go a little more general with your morning/ daily scripting. If Little Timmy is a couch potato who wouldn't know how to turn on a vacuum cleaner let alone clean the entire house, it's not worth scripting it out with him being the one who specifically does the amazing house cleaning. If you want to hand him some "paints and brushes" energy, maybe add into your Ten-Day Script a small, baby step such as, "Timmy has seemed interested in how the vacuum works lately. He is starting to actually seem curious about how to clean." If you aren't sure who will call you from the theater to offer you the job, but you really want the job, just say that someone from the theater called.

Now, that said, if you are specifically working on something that deals unequivocally with a specific person, put them in your script by name. For example, if you are going through a divorce and need your soon-to-be ex to be cooperative, then by all means, write it out. If you have your eye on someone special, and you want them to be in your life or ask you out (and you can believe and feel good about it when you write it down each day until it happens), *then write it out specifically.* Scripting really is flexible like that.

You will feel it. Seriously, you will feel it in your stomach or your heart or your head (or all three) if it is right or if it is pushing a little too hard. Just go with what you want and charge ahead full force. If it feels a little off or out of alignment, then back off and write it more generally. Also, when in doubt about including someone else or if it really makes you uncomfortable to do so, then just write about YOU and how you "felt" when whatever the other person did actually "happened."

The thing with scripting is that you have to be a little brave and willing to push through some of your own boundaries. I promise you, it works when you do it, so just go for it and find your own right place when it comes to including others in your script. I will tell you that the people who script most effectively include others by name when it feels right and include others in a general sense when it doesn't. It just works better.

Question: What happens if I miss a Daily Script, a Nightly Journal, or a Ten-Day Script? Do I have to start all over?

Answer: Nothing happens, and there is no starting over. There are a lot of myths out there about forming new habits. The thing is, scripting isn't so much a habit as it is a way of life. That may sound corny, but it is true. It's just something that you do every day. I will say this about missing a day: don't panic. But if you remember, still write your Nightly Journal. If you miss your Nightly Journal, that's okay too! I don't recommend missing it often, but if it happens, you don't lose progress. Just do your Daily Script the next day as usual.

One anecdotal thing I have noticed is that if you usually write your Ten-Day Script on Sunday, and you forget to do it one week, it is better to wait until the following Sunday to write your next Ten-Day Script. I have no idea why this is the case, but I have found in my years of doing this myself and teaching friends and family about scripting that if you usually write a Ten-Day Script on a Sunday and then one week write it on a Monday instead, it seems to mess with the overall flow. If life happens or something comes up or you are sick or you just forget to write your Ten-Day Script one week, again, DON'T PANIC. Just continue with your Daily Script and write your Ten-Day Script the following Sunday as usual. If you miss a Ten-Day Script, and you really feel good about writing it the next day, then do it, but still do your next Ten-Day Script six days later on Sunday.

If you start to forget or have missed writing your Ten-Day Script on your chosen day at least twice, pick a new day and start writing your Ten-Day Script every week on whatever the new day is. Try Wednesday. If that doesn't work, try Friday. You will find the right flow for writing your Ten-Day Script that works with your life and schedule. Don't panic if this happens when you are just getting started. And don't panic if this happens after you've been doing it for years. Scripting always finds a place in our lives, and there is always time for it, so don't beat yourself up if you need to make an adjustment.

The only requirement in all of this is that the Daily Script be done in the morning—*whatever that means to you*. Put a better way, your Daily Script needs to be done at the start of *your* day. If you are a slot attendant who works the graveyard shift at a casino, then do your script when you first wake up for your day at 8:00 p.m. Scripting is really flexible that way.

Question: Do I *have* to write this out in a notebook? Can I use my tablet notebook? Can I type it on my computer?

Answer: The easy answer to this question is that you can script with any medium you choose, but I have found notebooks—the paper ones—have served me well over the years. There are a few reasons for this. When we write in a physical notebook in the morning and then in a physical journal at night, we tend to be more focused on what we are doing than when we are typing on a computer or on our phone. It is also easier to separate the two: your scripting journal (where you keep your Daily Want List, Daily Belief List, and Daily Script/Ten-Day Script) and your Nightly Journal. Typing is also faster than writing for most, which means our focus—that crucial time when we are altering our world—is shortened from maybe five to ten minutes with handwriting to about two to three minutes with typing. The more time spent, which equals pure focus if you're scripting correctly, the faster results occur, in my experience. Everyone is different, however, and having a notebook makes it a little more like a ritual, plus it serves as a physical reminder to script and journal daily.

Now, that said, Solly recently got an iPad Pro and an Apple Pencil. He downloaded a free notebook app (there are tons of them) and he now uses the notepad and pencil to write his scripts and his journal. He is able to have many "notebooks" in the app, so it easy for him to separate the journal from the scripting notebook. He is still taking the same amount of time as he would if he was writing on physical paper because he is using the Apple Pencil; therefore it is almost equal to the paper version, and his results have been just as fantastic.

About two years ago I switched from writing out my Daily Wants and Daily Beliefs in my scripting notebook to typing them into another free notebook app on my laptop. I still write my Daily and Ten-Day Scripts and my Nightly Journal in paper notebooks/journals. There is just something about scripting on paper that has a magic for me. But everyone is different. I have had people use their laptops for a period of time and then switch to paper. I have had friends only ever use their word processor, and they have wonderful results. Again, though, I will add that the focus time is less, and there is creation power in the physical act of putting pen or pencil to paper. More recently I have experimented writing all of my scripts on my own iPad, and the results are indistinguishable from the handwritten scripts.

I have a friend who uses the notepad app in her smart phone, and she does great with her scripting. I would recommend that you start off with a paper notebook and journal, and if it really becomes unbearable, then find your digital tool of choice—some sort of smart tablet that has a stylus or "pencil" would be where I would go next, if you can (many relatively inexpensive ones can be found on Amazon, and even the older tablets that didn't used to have a pencil feature when they were released now have stylus pencils for sale that are compatible with them!).

If you decide to start out in a word processor on your computer and aren't having success, switch to paper notebooks/journals for a few weeks. That usually solves any problem people tend to have.

If you remember, my friend Mitch mentioned our trip to Disneyland in the foreword of this book. He referred to my partner Solly's script from that day and journal from that night. Like Mitch said, save one minor detail (a small gift Mitch bought for us), the Daily Script that Solly wrote that morning and Solly's journal from that night before bed were almost completely interchangeable! Solly wrote both of them on his iPad Pro with his pencil, and it's hard to tell the difference between them and scans or copies from a notebook.

For fun, and to show you what Mitch was talking about, here are Solly's Daily Script (page 149) followed by Solly's journal from that night right before we went to bed (page 150).

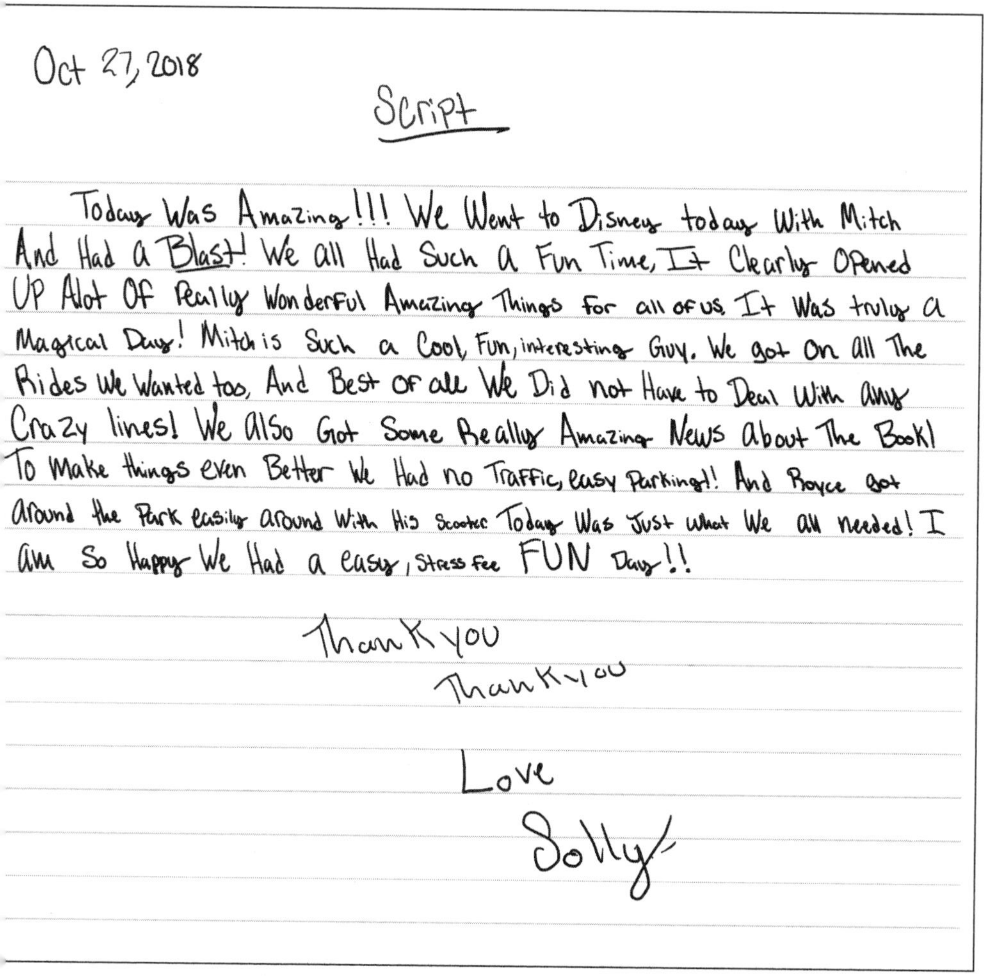

Oct 27, 2018

Script

Today Was Amazing!!! We Went to Disney today With Mitch And Had a Blast! We all Had Such a Fun Time, It Clearly Opened Up Alot Of Really Wonderful Amazing Things for all of us It Was truly a Magical Day! Mitch is Such a Cool, Fun, interesting Guy. We got On all The Rides We Wanted too, And Best of all We Did not Have to Deal With any Crazy lines! We also Got Some Really Amazing News about The Book! To Make things even Better We Had no Traffic, easy Parking!! And Royce got Around the Park easily around With His Scooter Today Was Just what We all needed! I am So Happy We Had a easy, Stress Free FUN Day!!

Thank You
    Thank You

        Love

            Solly

Fig. 8.1. Solly's Daily Script, October 27, 2018 (Solly Hemus)

A few notes about Solly's script, for those who are curious:

This was the first time Solly and Mitch had spent a real, full day together, so Solly was excited and nervous to spend time with someone he knew meant so much to me (in the best way possible!).

I had a busted medial tendon in my ankle at the time, so that is the scooter he refers to (though it was a knee scooter, and we didn't use a wheelchair to cut lines at all).

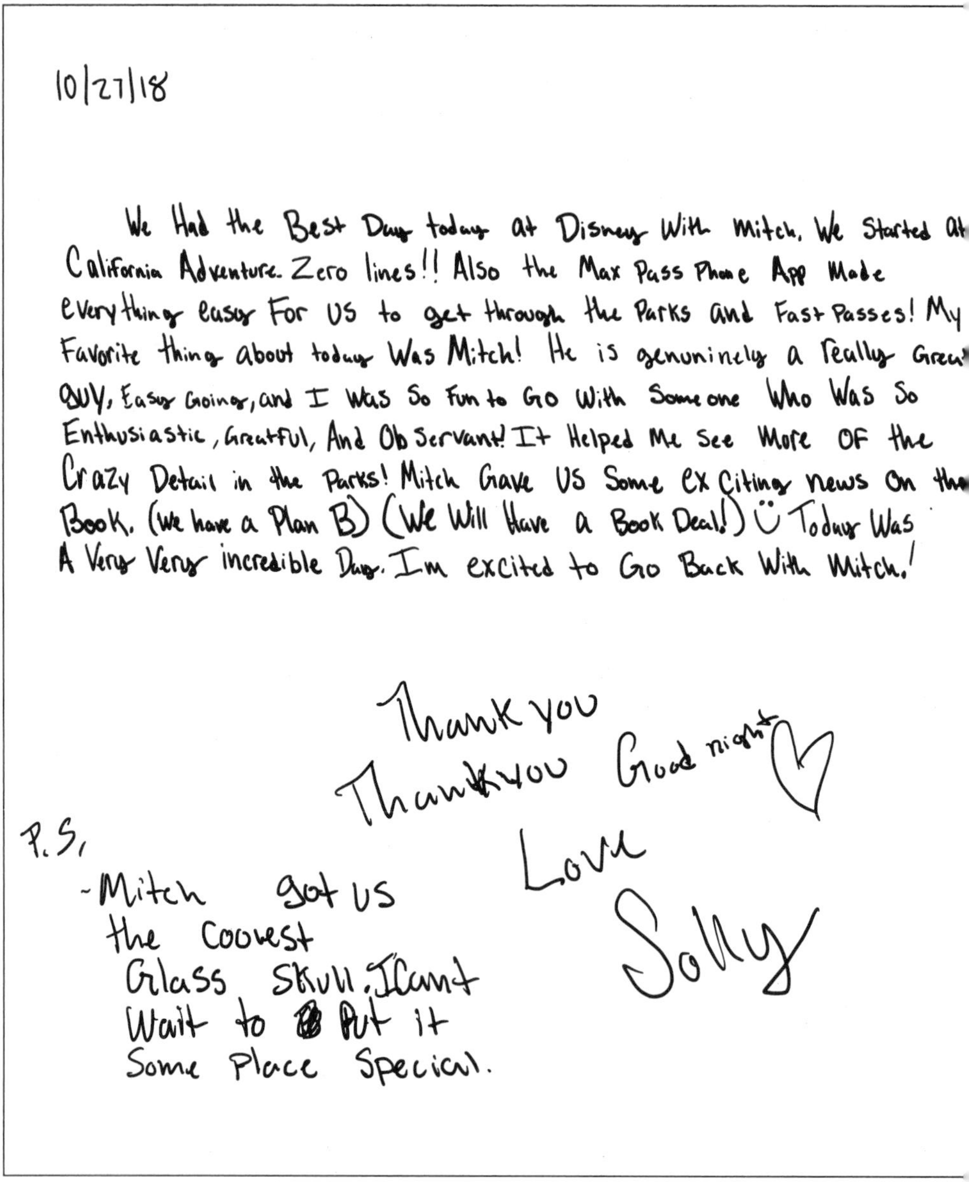

10/27/18

We Had the Best Day today at Disney With Mitch, We Started at California Adventure. Zero lines!! Also the Max Pass Phone App Made everything easy For us to get through the Parks and Fast Passes! My Favorite thing about today Was Mitch! He is genuinely a really Great Guy, Easy Going, and I Was So Fun to Go With Someone Who Was So Enthusiastic, Greatful, And Ob Servant! It Helped Me See More OF the Crazy Detail in the Parks! Mitch Gave US Some eX citing news On the Book. (We have a Plan B) (We Will Have a Book Deal!) ☺ Today Was A Very Very incredible Day. I'm excited to Go Back With Mitch.!

Thank you
Thank you Good night ♡
Love
Solly

P.S,
-Mitch got us
the Coolest
Glass Skull. I Cant
Wait to Put it
Some Place Special.

Fig. 8.2. Solly's Nightly Journal, October 27, 2018 (Solly Hemus)

The book Solly refers to is the first book I wrote. Mitch gave me some great news about a publisher who was very interested in looking at it if the one who had been reading it decided to not make a deal with me.

All of that aside, you can see how indistinguishable the iPad notebook is from a paper notebook, so, that would be my second choice if paper just really isn't your thing.

Question: HELP! Scripting has been going amazingly for me, and now it stopped working/stalled/slowed down. What do I do?
Answer: First of all—breathe. Scripting, especially the first few months after you begin, can have good and bad days or even weeks. If you've been doing well with your scripting (and things have been going great), and then it all seems to stop, a couple of things need to be looked at and adjusted: your morning routine and your focus.

Your Morning Routine

Your morning routine (and everything that it entails) is almost *always* part of the problem if scripting seems to suddenly stop or stall. Take inventory of what your morning looks like: Are you waking up and looking at your phone, computer, newspaper, or television? If so, STOP. You should wake up, use the bathroom if needed (and brush your teeth), grab a snack or some water if you want, and *immediately* grab your notebook and do your Daily Want List, followed by your Daily Belief List and then your Daily Script (or wait if it is a Sunday when you write your Ten-Day Script in the evening). It is crucial that you remain undisturbed and undistracted when you wake up. If you have screaming kids, or a snoring partner, get up earlier or try going into a room where you won't be disturbed for twenty minutes so you can focus and do your morning routine.

I had a friend who had two children. Her scripting was going great the first week, but then she soon started to allow herself to check her phone notifications when she woke up—an old habit creeping back. She stopped doing that, but her scripting was still not as aligned as it was when she first started. She then realized that she was waking up and letting her mind automatically get into the "go" mode of what she had to do for her kids.

They also liked to be near her the moment she woke up. So she ended up taking her notebook and some headphones into the bathroom with her. She also woke up a few minutes earlier than she had been. Within one day she noticed that her scripting was back on track.

Another friend of mine got into a relationship with a girl just a few weeks after he started scripting daily for the first time. He was having amazing results. Then he found out that his new girlfriend thought scripting was weird. He realized that whenever he would stay at her house or she would stay at his, he wasn't scripting a full page or he would hide or rush the script. He was falling in love with this girl and was feeling conflicted.

I told him to wake up at 4:00 a.m. every day for a week. He knew his girlfriend wouldn't wake up at that time. He ended up not only doing his morning scripting routine but also used his new extra time to meditate and work out. His scripting immediately began to work again. As it turns out, despite thinking I was insane for suggesting that he wake up at 4:00 a.m., he ended up loving it, and he now wakes up that early every day. He is still with his lovely girlfriend, who became his fiancée and, as it turned out, is now an avid fan of scripting!

Why did I tell him to wake up so early? It wasn't to hide what he was doing from his girlfriend; I knew that her opinion of scripting wasn't the issue. It was his feeling of not having the space to do it without feeling weird that was causing the problem. Sometimes our brains need to be shocked into something different—and waking up at 4:00 a.m. was a huge, positive shock to his brain.

Waking up this early allowed him to be still and not worry about replying to emails or checking his phone too. No one expects you to reply to them at 4:00 a.m.! Solly and I have been waking up at 4:00 a.m. every day for a few years, and we both love it! We sometimes will wake up at 3:00 a.m. or even 2:00 a.m. to do the "script shock" for our brains if we feel like our scripting is starting to lag. Don't let this scare you though . . . if your normal wake-up time is 10:00 a.m., and you're having trouble with your scripting, then just wake up at 8:00 a.m. for a week. All of this is adjustable and an option to try if your scripting success seems to have suddenly slowed.

Your Focus

If you adjust your morning routine and are still having issues with getting your scripting to work or it seems to be lagging or it hasn't started making a noticeable impact, the answer may be your focus. Some people need to do some extra exercises at certain times to shift their minds slightly so that they are putting their attention (and therefore energy) onto what they want for a little bit longer each morning.

There are a few exercises that help you to not only extend your focused energy but also to come up with new and exciting things to add into your Daily Script and Ten-Day Script. Push yourself to write fifty or even a hundred intentions on your Daily Want List. You may think this seems impossible, but it is actually pretty easy. I refer to this process as the "Cobweb Clearer" because, in pushing yourself to write more and more intentions, you tend to get all of the more routine or boring wants out of the way within the first twenty-five to thirty intentions that you write down. From there you must push your imagination and not be afraid to think BIG. Imagine your wildest dreams and even things you absolutely think may be impossible, then write them down on your mega list! This process of pushing has an incredible impact on scripting, because it allows you to see how many wonderful things are just waiting for you to manifest.

Another focus exercise that tends to unstick people is what I call the Peter Pan List. This one is really fun and easy and can be done in place of your Daily Want List or in addition to your daily work. With the Peter Pan List, you write down as many of the things that you wanted as a child or teenager as you can remember. Did you want to be a rock star? Did you want to be a president or prime minister? Did you beg your parents for a pony or hot rod? Whatever wants—big or small—you had as a child, you write down on this list. I would aim for around twenty items. Keep it light and fun. Don't write down anything that might make you feel negative or put you in a negative state of mind, such as "I wanted my dad to stay with my mom," "I wanted to have food on the table," and so on.

This list is formatted a bit differently from your other lists. Following is an example.

Peter Pan List—May 28, 2020

When I was young, I intended to . . .

- Have a beautiful horse
- Take a trip to Disneyland
- Be a movie star
- Have an older sister
- Get a new bike
- Have a brand-new Porsche
- Live in a huge mansion

A third powerful focusing exercise that will help you if you are stuck and/or having trouble getting started is called "Forty-Four Reasons Why." I learned a version of this exercise from Grabhorn's *Excuse Me, Your Life Is Waiting Playbook* and made some adjustments over the years to make it my own. This is fairly simple and can be adjusted and played with quite a bit. For this exercise, you are going to pick an intention from your Daily Want List and, on a new page, write down forty-four reasons why you want the want! I'm not going to sugarcoat it; this is hard at first for some people. You MUST push yourself, however, as this exercise really elevates your mood, enhances your focus, and gives you tons of new ideas to incorporate into your Daily Script and your Ten-Day Script. You want to really stay positive here, asking yourself why and answering "because, because, because . . ."! At the top of the page under the heading, copy the intention you have chosen from your Daily Want List and write "Why?" below it. Following is an idea of what the first nine reasons on a Forty-Four Reasons Why list should look like.

Forty-Four Reasons Why—December 26, 2022

I intend for every book of mine that is published to be a critically acclaimed, commercially successful #1 national and international bestseller.

Why?

1. Because I love the feeling of validation I get from having people enjoy my writing.

2. Because the success of the books I write means that I will be able to provide more information and more books to the world.

3. Because I love the sense of pride I get when my hard work is recognized by people I look up to and respect.

4. Because it makes me feel excited.

5. Because when people respond to my writing in a positive way, that means they are really getting use out of the information contained in the books I write, and it is having a positive impact on their lives, which makes me feel warm and fuzzy inside!

6. Because writing about New Thought is my lifelong passion and having it recognized feels wonderful.

7. Because I love the feeling of relief I get from knowing I am helping people better themselves.

8. Because it is fulfilling knowing that people all over the world are using these tools to make the world a better place.

9. Because being able to say I have a #1 bestselling book is exciting! I love the way it makes me feel.

It is important to think of the want as having already been accomplished when you are writing about why you want it. I know that sounds weird, but the example is pretty clear. You may not have a critically acclaimed, commercially successful #1 national and international bestselling book yet, but you can certainly ask yourself, "Why do I want this?" and your "because" answers will rapidly put you into the emotional, mental, feeling place of having that want already. If you've had a #1 bestseller before, draw on the positives of that experience when doing your list.

Now, I mentioned that you can adjust this exercise. A variation that I love and is tons of fun uses the same principle, but with more items from your Daily Want List and fewer answers to the question "Why?" For this version, choose about five to seven intentions from your Daily Want List. Then aim to write five "because" reasons below each intention. This is an excellent way to really get into the feeling place of having your intentions, and it puts you in the perfect headspace for your scripting.

Another recommendation I would give to anyone feeling stuck is that if you've been handwriting everything, try switching to your laptop or whatever you use to type. If you have been using a laptop (or tablet, phone, etc.), switch to doing your daily work in notebooks and physical journals. This is the other most common way to solve any issue with scripting.

And remember: you don't have to be stuck or struggling to do any of the things I mention above! Even if things are going great with your daily scripting and lists, you absolutely should experiment a little! Play around. If you've been having great luck using a notebook, try typing on your laptop or use your tablet for a few days. Does your scripting get better, stay the same, or stall?

Find your own, awesome balance in all of this and have fun with it. Scripting can take anywhere from a few days to a few months to line up with your Nightly Journal, so don't beat yourself up if it isn't happening yet. It will—I promise.

A TYPICAL WEEK OF SCRIPTING

Scripting is really very simple, yet the changes and amazing things that come into your life are beyond ordinary. So what does a typical day and week of scripting look like? The first thing you want to do is consider time. Ask yourself this question: "When does my day (or 'morning') begin?" As we talked about earlier, some people work weird hours. If you work the night or graveyard shift and wake up at 5:00 p.m. every day, then your morning starts at 5:00 p.m. If you are in school or have normal work hours, then your morning may begin around 6:00 a.m. every day. If you don't work or are retired, then your morning may begin at 11:00 a.m. There is no wrong answer to the question "When does my day begin?"

What I recommend is, when you begin implementing scripting into your daily life, start by setting your alarm clock twenty to forty minutes earlier than usual. Why such a drastic difference? Because we all write at different speeds. Also, some people may want to do longer Daily Want Lists—which is awesome! I recommend that you start off simply. On a work or school day, set your alarm to go off about thirty minutes earlier than normal (yes, this might suck at first, but when you start to notice all of the awesome changes in your life, it won't seem so bad). Then get out of bed and RESIST THE URGE TO CHECK YOUR PHONE. In fact, when you wake up, resist all urges to check your phone or email or to turn on the radio or television. TRUST ME—it matters. If you usually get up and use the bathroom and brush your teeth first thing, then do that. Then, before you do anything else, get out your scripting notebook. Remember: This is your time. You want your head unclogged and not full of the day yet, because you are setting up what your day is going to be like. It is important not to let the news or voicemails or emails get in the way.

For the first few days, write anywhere from five to seven wants and one to three beliefs using a different page for each thing. So: one page with "Wants" written at the top, a new page for "Beliefs," and then your Daily Script on the next page. Don't cram everything together! This is important. If your first day happens to be a Sunday, then just do a normal one-page Daily Script and do your Ten-Day Script the following Sunday.

Then, every night, right before you turn off the lights (your phone should already be away for the night), write in your Nightly Journal. Write out your day exactly as it really happened. It may take anywhere from a few days to a few weeks (sometimes a month or two) for your Daily Script to start matching your Nightly Journal, but hang in there. The magic really starts when the two begin matching up!

If it's a weekend or a day off where you normally sleep in, that is fine. You don't need to worry about setting your alarm as long as you can put aside the time to write your Daily Want List, Daily Belief List, and Daily Script (if it's a Ten-Day Script day, then you don't have to write your script first thing, but you can). A typical week looks like this:

> **Sunday, April 2:** Wake up and write your Daily Want List and Daily Belief List. At some point during the day before bed, write out your Ten-Day Script dated April 12th (ten days ahead). Then write your Nightly Journal before bed.
>
> **Monday, April 3–Saturday, April 8:** Wake up and write your Daily Want List, Daily Belief List, and Daily Script in morning and your Nightly Journal before bed.
>
> **Sunday, April 9:** Wake up and write your Daily Want List and Daily Belief List. At some point during the day before bed, write out your Ten-Day Script dated April 19th (ten days ahead). Then write your Nightly Journal before bed.

It is really easy and simple, and you will absolutely notice shifts and changes happening rapidly in your life. Some people get bored with the Daily Want List and Daily Belief List. I feel like we can always write at least a few wants as intentions. It helps to focus us . . . and I encourage everyone to do this for the first two-and-half months. If, at that point, it is just too much for you, start with dropping the Belief List, then, if you must, the Daily Want List. This should go without saying, but I'll say it anyway: never drop your Daily Script or your Ten-Day Script—they are crucial, and not just for manifesting. Science backs up the fact that journaling in general is good for you! As an article on PsychCentral says:

> [Journaling] has a positive impact on physical well-being. University of Texas at Austin psychologist and researcher James Pennebaker contends that regular journaling strengthens immune cells, called T-lymphocytes. Other research indicates that journaling decreases the symptoms of asthma and rheumatoid arthritis. Pennebaker

believes that writing about stressful events helps you come to terms with them, acting as a stress management tool, thus reducing the impact of these stressors on your physical health.[3]

Scripting incorporates all of the benefits of journaling and goal setting and takes it into a whole new realm.

If nothing above works to solve any stuck feeling or slowness you are experiencing with scripting—or if you are having no success at all—the next chapter will provide the ultimate medicine to solve this problem. The "big guns," as it were.

One of the things that you must understand before we begin to wrap up our journey into scripting is also the most crucial: Scripting (along with your Daily Want List, Belief List, etc.) is one of the most effective tools we have in our arsenal for combatting mind viruses, or memes. The science behind memetics is something that is crucial to understand if you have even a casual interest in manifesting and creating your reality. Memes aren't just cute or funny little pictures people share online. The study of memetics is not some silly pseudoscientific fluff. It is a serious business and is something that large corporations and even the military use in their strategies.

Nine

The Sword of Scripting

It has forever been thus: So long as men write what they think, then all of the other freedoms—all of them—may remain intact. And it is then that writing becomes a weapon of truth, an article of faith, an act of courage.

ROD SERLING

WHEN I FIRST STARTED SEEING REAL RESULTS and success from scripting, I was elated. It was actually on set of Disney Channel's *Wizards of Waverly Place* when I had a strange thought that felt like I was asking myself a "dirty" question. I didn't love that I was even questioning anything going on in my life, since I was literally living one of my dreams come true in that moment. But I wondered why, despite things going so well in most areas, there were still a few really bad things happening in my life.

A few weeks into filming, my personal life was in upheaval on many fronts, and then my mentor died suddenly. For all of the wonderful things I was manifesting into my life, I couldn't wrap my head around why some weird, out-of-place, bad things were happening. Some may say, "Life happens" or "You can't control everything," and I get that, but my intuition said something else was at play.

It was 2007, and, as you know, I had just spent almost five years discovering scripting and manifesting the right way. I spent the following ten years searching for the answer to a simple question: "Is there another factor, something other than the traditional models of 'manifesting,' at play in our lives when it comes to our experience?" It took a decade, but I finally figured it out—and it changed everything for me and my life in the best way possible.

The answer is yes, there is another form of creation, and it affects each and every single one of us—most of the time without us even being aware of its existence! What had I discovered? Memetics and memes. Well, I didn't "discover" them, of course, but what I did figure out is that memes are the missing key to manifesting. I want to give you a short but powerful understanding of memetics. This is so that you can be sure you are using your newfound "magic wand" (scripting) to its fullest potential.

New Thought has needed an answer to quite a few problems over the past century, and, while this doesn't solve all of the issues, I believe including memes and memetics into the discussion is a step forward. Understanding memes and how they influence and affect every single area of your life and your surroundings is crucial to your experience here on Earth. So . . . what are they?

ME, ME, MEMES

Over the past few years we have been conditioned to believe that a meme is an online picture or image with some funny words superimposed onto it. Those online images are both the memes themselves and the *result* of memes, yet to believe that they in any way are all there is to memes is severely shortsighted.

The best definition of *meme* comes from Brodie's book *Virus of the Mind:*

> The meme, which rhymes with "beam," is the basic building block of culture in the same way the gene is the basic building block of life. Memes are not only the building blocks of culture on a large scale—making up cultures, languages, and religions—but also on a

small scale: memes are the building blocks of your mind, the programming of your mental "computer."[1]

Reread that last line, because it is something you must understand
on a fundamental level: *Memes are the building blocks of your mind, the
programming of your mental computer.*

Memetics is the study of how memes replicate, interact with other
memes, and evolve. Memes are best thought of as being alive. Scientists
and researchers refer to memes as "mind viruses" because they have
discovered that memes are contagious.[2] Unlike a physical virus spread
through the air or by physical means, memes are spread easily through
communication and culture.

The term *meme* was originally coined in the 1970s by controversial
English evolutionary scientist Richard Dawkins in his groundbreaking
book *The Selfish Gene.* It was derived from the Greek word *mimeme*
(pronounced like "my meme"), which literally means "imitated thing"
or something that is imitated.

The idea of memes started going viral (as successful memes tend to
do) after *The Selfish Gene* was released in 1976. Memes are not children of the internet revolution, as is commonly thought. They've been
around since humanity began. They just weren't given a proper name
until the 1970s (like our new word *Nexus,* this is another example of the
importance of labeling things when there are no words). Governments
around the world have even created entire texts devoted to memetic
warfare—for real.

Scientists explain that through imitation—for example, sounds
(which became words) and movements (hugs, holding hands, waving,
etc.)—humans had a cultural evolution alongside our physical one. This
is something that continues to this day: through imitation, our culture
evolves. Basically memetics, at its most basic level, explains why humans
enjoy art, dancing, building theme parks, and so on. Otherwise, from
a strict evolutionary standpoint (think "survival of the fittest"), those
behaviors and actions make no sense.

But throw in memes and memetics, which states that humans, from early man all the way up to modern people of today (you and me), don't only have genes dictating their bodies but *also* have memes dictating their behaviors, and suddenly you have an explanation. Memes are like viruses, and viruses have only one function: to spread and replicate.

Dawkins's original explanation of a meme is as follows:

Examples of memes are tunes, ideas, catch-phrases, clothes fashions, ways of making pots or building arches. Just as genes propagate themselves in the gene pool by leaping from body to body via sperm or eggs, so memes propagate themselves in the meme pool by leaping from brain to brain via a process which, in the broad sense, can be called imitation. If a scientist hears, or reads about, a good idea, he passes it onto his colleagues and students. He mentions it in his articles and lectures. If the idea catches on, it can be said to propagate itself, spreading from brain to brain.[3]

Dawkins goes on to explain:

Memes should be regarded as living structures, not just metaphorically, but technically. When you plant a fertile meme in my mind you literally parasitize my brain, turning it into a vehicle for the meme's propagation in just the way a virus may parasitize the genetic mechanism of the host cell.[4]

Memes began evolving at a feverish rate at the beginning of the twenty-first century with the availability of the personal computer and internet and the subsequent technological revolution. People began sharing information and ideas at a rate never before experienced in human history. Truly, anything can be a meme, but it's the things that "stick" (or catch on) that cause real change. Think of anything that has gone viral in the past fifteen years, and you are thinking about a meme. Even a person can be a meme. Madonna, Britney Spears, and Kim Kardashian are good examples.

Memes are in a constant state of change. They are viral units or pieces of culture that spread rapidly through a society. These can be trends that include anything from bell bottoms to microwave dinners. Memes, however, have a poisonous side and include cycles of inner-city poverty, millions of families that only eat at unhealthy fast-food chains, and even terrorism copycat attacks. When you look out into the world and see most of the people around you fitting in, staring at screens, doing what they can to keep up, you aren't watching zombies, you are watching people infected with hundreds of thousands of memes.

When memetics was put forth as a scientific realm of study, one of the most shocking things that researchers discovered was that *our thoughts don't always come from us.* Brodie states:

> Your thoughts are not always your own original ideas. You catch thoughts—you get infected with them, both directly from other people and indirectly from viruses of the mind. People don't seem to like the idea that they aren't in control of their thoughts. The reluctance of people to even consider this notion is probably the main reason the scientific work done so far is not better known.[5]

The implications of this are staggering. Thoughts create the emotions that create the frequencies and vibrations that draw things into our lives. *If we are manipulated, via memes, into thinking thoughts that are NOT our own, and we can't recognize this, it becomes clear that we may not always be in charge of what manifests in our lives—of what we are selecting from the Nexus.* One of the most incredible things about scripting is that it forces our brain to focus, which is supremely helpful in eliminating harmful memes. And people who understand memes will have an advantage in life that billions of other people currently do not possess.

Remember when we talked about how our reticular activating system has the ability to be programmed to show us what we want to see, as well as Donald Hoffman's discovery that evolution does not favor reality? Our brains are always working to create our perception much like, as Hoffman said, a computer works to create an interface like a desktop with icons. There are no real icons, just programmed data we perceive as a desktop with icons. Memes fit into this discovery nicely.

An easy way to understand memes is to think of them as the building blocks and programmers of your mind's "computer." Your mind forms the thoughts that form emotions and frequencies that bring your desires into physical form via selecting from the field we learned about earlier and are now calling the Nexus. Your mind is the starting point from which you create whatever it is you want in your life. Once you know this, then you can understand how incredibly important having a basic understanding of memes is to creating your reality. Especially when we understand that science says that memes can cause us to have thoughts that aren't even our own, without even realizing this is the case!

Memes can be positive and negative. Brushing your teeth, meditating, and exercise are all beneficial memes. You see, when memes are positive pieces of culture that are not harmful and that we enjoy, there isn't a problem. But when memes are negative and act as harmful viruses of the mind, they can cause us to act in destructive ways that can hurt not just us but also others.

Remember in the previous chapter, when I brought up the topic of adding other people into your script? For those of you who are students of New Thought, where we are taught that you can't create in another's experience, understanding memetics is going to most likely shift your opinion on that commonly taught rule.

These meme mind viruses succeed by programming our brains to believe that the meme must remain alive, regardless of what it means to our own personal health, happiness, and well-being. That includes making others behave and do things that they might not normally be compelled to do in their normal lives. Advertisers tell us that Listerine is the absolute best mouthwash, so millions of people buy and use the product, but the thought of buying and using Listerine is not our own, no matter how hard that may be to rationalize to ourselves.

The tenets of New Thought state that we cannot create in another's reality, but that is not completely true if we are being manipulated by memes to think thoughts that we cannot even distinguish from our own. This explains why, in probably more cases than we can ever truly know, bad things can and do happen in life. Memes don't explain all bad things, but they can explain some things, which is a start.

Understanding memetics and how it has affected the abilities of people who want to create the life of their dreams requires changing the way we think about manifesting, science, spirituality, and life in general. It may sound complicated, but it's not; anyone can do what is needed to shift their belief system for the better. Rest assured: *scripting (which includes your Daily Want List, Belief List, Ten-Day Script, etc.) is one of the most powerful tools in our arsenal for reprogramming memes.*

Science has discovered that memes and mind viruses appear in the following three ways:

1. They can come into existence spontaneously.
2. They can be spread and appear through communication.
3. They can be created intentionally.

It's not that hard to understand what the power of a meme could be. In scripting you are literally creating new memes to delete and/or override old memes that don't serve you. You are spontaneously bringing forth new ideas (memes) into existence via a means of communication to yourself—writing your script—and you are doing this intentionally. Scripting the correct way, as you have learned to do throughout this book, harnesses the power of memes.

So where can memes be found? Well, memes exist in a few places. The two most inhabited spaces are the real, physical world and cyberspace. One of the modern-day authorities on memes, Susan Blackmore, has a great example of an actual, easy-to-understand real-world meme in action: toilet paper.

Walk into the Belmond Hotel Monasterio, a five-star hotel in Peru, and you will find this:

Fig. 9.1. Belmond Hotel Monasterio toilet paper
(photo by Jayegirl99)

Then take a plane across the world and walk into a public bathroom in Papeete, Tahiti, French Polynesia, and you can find this (a memetic variation, but still a meme of the same "species"):

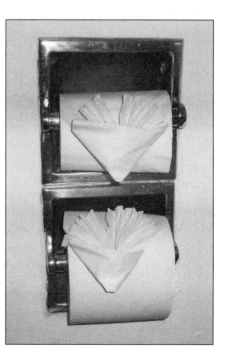

Fig. 9.2. Toilet paper
origami in Papeete, Tahiti
(photo by Richard Faulder)

Now head over to the United States, and, like magic, you may find this at a Ritz Carlton hotel:

*Fig. 9.3. Toilet paper rose at the Ritz Carlton
(photo by Aaron Gustafson)*

You can find this strange phenomenon all over the world! What purpose does it serve? Why do we fold the toilet paper that way? I know even I have been guilty of cleaning my bathroom and doing this spontaneously. It has no value, except maybe to tell the next person that the bathroom has been cleaned (or, worse, that someone else has recently been in the bathroom).

This is a classic example of a meme: *a cultural habit or act of mimicking that is so embedded in society that no one thinks to question its purpose.* Memes and memetics explain things that "go viral." You could say this weird little cultural trend of folding toilet paper into an artsy shape is *something* (a meme, which acts like a virus) *that became popular* (went viral, or "infected" millions of people by becoming embedded in the psyche of humankind, as memes tend to do), *and now is something we are all used to doing and seeing without question.*

I know you are probably asking, "What the hell does toilet paper have to do with creating the life of my dreams?" Well, a lot, actually. Whether they arise spontaneously, are created intentionally, or are birthed and spread through communication, all memes have one thing in common: *As soon as a meme is birthed, it begins a life that is independent of its creator. It then sets out to "infect" as many other people as possible.*

In his book *Thought Contagion,* Aaron Lynch explains memes the following way:

> Overlooked by establishment social sciences, thought contagion warrants more attention as a force shaping society. *Like a software virus in a computer network or a physical virus in a city, thought contagions proliferate by effectively "programming" for their own retransmission* [emphasis mine]. Beliefs affect retransmission in so many ways that they set off a colorful, unplanned growth race among diverse "epidemics"' of ideas. Actively contagious ideas are now called memes.[6]

One final passage from Brodie now seems appropriate:

> Read a newspaper? Catch a mind virus. Listen to the radio? Catch a mind virus. Hang out with your friends and shoot the breeze about nothing in particular? Catch one mind virus after another. If your life isn't going the way you would like, you can bet mind viruses are playing a large part. Having relationship problems? Mind viruses take over parts of your brain and divert them from what would give you long-term happiness. Having trouble in your job or career? Mind viruses cloud your future and steer you along a career path that supports their agenda, not your quality of life.[7]

Marketers, knowingly and unknowingly, will use common branding tools to make consumers (you and me) *want* to buy their product to make it a part of our actual identity. As the process of branding any product builds, we consumers become more and more a part of the product's story. The method the marketers use to sink the meme of the brand into our fabric is layered. Often it can be through emotional triggers that cause us to feel a vacuum that we need to fill. Most of the time, this perceived need can be satisfied only, in our new memetic belief, by purchasing the product, like, say, a new toilet bowl cleaner. The best branding builds a relationship between the consumer and the product where the consumer is the star of the show.

Like I said before, memes are your mind's computer instructions. It may seem counterintuitive, but *the key to being free is to use the tools of memetic control on ourselves.* It is easier than you think to turn the tables and begin selecting and censoring what memes we are and are not exposed to and who we interact with on a daily basis and learn to finally regain control of our own minds. Scripting can help or even outright accomplish this for you. Scripting is the sword that slashes through the memes that are not serving you.

Since I began harnessing the power of memes and combining them with my New Thought and manifesting actions, my life has become full of joy and marvelous manifestations. Uninstalling the viruses from my inner computer has truly been life transforming—from manifesting large sums of money in the span of a few weeks to helping a friend overcome her memetic blocks so she could lose thirty pounds. Memes are the gears in today's age that make all of the other concepts ever taught in New Thought studies move, function, and work for us! We just didn't know it . . . until now.

Things I have wanted and worked on creating in my life that would take years to manifest in the past now appear within days, sometimes hours! Those of you out there who are already experts at using manifesting and New Thought teachings to create things know the agony and frustration of failed deliberate creations. You know the heartache that we never talk about but that often accompanies unfulfilled manifestations. You know about the secret mental, physical, and emotional exhaustion that often occurs after years of trying to manifest something unsuccessfully.

For me, discovering that there actually was a real scientifically backed field of study (memetics) that explained all of the "dirty questions" I was asking was the biggest relief in the world. My wish is for you too to feel this relief and excitement. I had only just figured out scripting when I was questioning why some bad things were still occurring in my life. A decade after finding memes, and learning how to use them to create, I found myself laughing because I had one of the biggest tools for clearing old memes and creating new ones at my disposal the whole time: scripting.

With scripting, you do the following:

- Identify the memes that have infected you and your life.
- Turn the goals and desires you wish to bring into your life into memes.
- Throw away the old memes or rewire useful ones to serve your goals and desires.
- Combine the tools of manifesting with memes (your Daily Script and Daily Want List, etc.) to make change happen in your life.
- Learn how to make strong meme signals using scripting and a secret tool I'm about to lay out.

WHAT IS THE LANGUAGE OF YOUR MIND?

Let me ask you a question: Do you think in words? Really think about it for a moment. The short answer is no . . . and yes. According to some studies, about 25 percent of our thinking is us talking to ourselves in our mind. The other 75 percent is us thinking in pictures. That is nothing to be ashamed of but rather something that should be embraced.

On the conscious level, we are more apt to think in both words and pictures, but when it comes to the subconscious, we are biologically programmed to think only in pictures. We had images in our mind long before we had words. In fact the first forms of communication were pictures, or pictographs, painted on cave walls. In the context of human existence, the written word and spoken word are relatively new advancements.

While many scholars and New Thought teachers agree that pictures and symbols are the language of the subconscious, they often leave it out of their literature, to the (accidental) detriment of their students.

A major reason that most people become frustrated with positive think-ing, the Law of Attraction, and New Thought boils down to one thing: they aren't even aware or conscious of the fact that the majority of their methods require you to speak a "foreign language"—namely, words—to your subconscious. When you are writing or saying affirmations, think-ing positive phrases (words rather than images), or simply studying, your subconscious cannot understand what you want it to do as easily as it would if you were speaking to it in images and symbols.

Did you ever notice that the entire Law of Attraction/New Thought methodology seems to work best when you infuse strong emotion and passion into your want? Add that passion to the image of your goal, and you will be on the right path to achieving it. Scripting does this, believe it or not, even though it is a process that uses words and writing.

Think of your subconscious as the most brilliant VCR in the world. No matter how good it is, inserting a DVD of a movie into it isn't going to make it play the movie. The same goes for the book the movie is based on—even if you could get it in there, the VCR is not going to show you images of the pages. It is the same principle with your sub-conscious mind (which, incidentally, is the most critical element you need to work with to manifest): it is a brilliant machine, but if you try to force it to "play" or understand a format it wasn't meant to translate, it will seem broken.

Think about this: When you hear the name Kim Kardashian, what immediately happens? Do you see a picture of her in your mind's eye? Or do you see the name "Kim Kardashian" written out in your head? The answer has been scientifically proved (unless you are an alien): If I say Kim Kardashian, you picture her in your mind. That is because she has infected you via memetics. As bad as that sounds, it actually isn't a bad thing at all—it just means that the Kardashians are meme creation geniuses.

The funny thing about knowing Kim Kardashian well enough to picture her is that the knowledge of her serves no biological or evolu-tionary purpose for her fans, or anyone, really. But just because memes serve no biological, primal purpose (when I say primal, I am referring to the basics: survival, food, procreation) doesn't mean that we can't use memetics to attain all of those goals and desires we've been working on for so long, does it? No!

In fact, for the first time ever, I'm going to reveal one of my most effective tools of creation. It is creation at its most exciting and explosive. It is "selecting from the Nexus" at its finest, and it is one of the things that will make you an "Apex Creator." I'm so excited to share the process with you.

Ten

Apex Creator

You can't forbid children to do things that are available to them at every turn. God told Eve, "Don't give the apple to Adam," and look what happened. It's in our nature to want the things we see.

EVEL KNIEVEL

THE PICTURE SCRIPT: A MASTER'S TOOL

Evel Knievel's words above are so powerful and true: it's in our nature to want the things we see. Scripting is a tool that makes you a meme mechanic, engineering your life around your own memes, not those of some corporation or other person. It allows you to access a field—the Nexus—and select from it the things you want to manifest, or see, in your life.

What if I told you there was one last scripting tool that allowed you to take what you now know about memes and memetics and combine it with your newfound, amazing scripting powers? It's something I've had in my proverbial back pocket for some time now, and let me tell you, this is scripting on steroids. It is powerful, fast, and works incredibly well. I call it the "Picture Script."

After you have done a minimum of two weeks of your scripting routine—meaning you have scripted every day, hopefully done your

Daily Want List/Daily Belief List, journaled every night, and have at least two Ten-Day Scripts under your belt—try this exercise. The results are very powerful. As I mentioned in chapter 8, if you are experiencing any issues with scripting, this process will snap everything back into action. But you don't have to be having any issues with scripting to do this exercise. I encourage you to play around with it whenever you feel like it because it is really fun, and the results are seriously out of this world.

The Picture Script is actually really simple. It takes a little time to prepare and actually complete (but it is so worth it—the results are just that cool). What you do here is mash together your knowledge of memes and scripting into one awesome thing! You have probably heard of vision boards. I do my own version, which relies heavily on what I have learned from memetics. But the Picture Script is a whole other animal, mixing ingredients from what I've learned in memetics, scripting, and the concept of a vision board.

First I want you to think about what you do when you write a Ten-Day Script. Let's expand on the thinking behind that process for a moment. Over the years Solly and my mom, Neva, and I have created some fun one-off variations based on the Ten-Day Script. These are completely optional, but you need to at least know about them before we get into the instructions for the Picture Script.

First of the Month Script

I love this script. The First of the Month Script is a ONE PAGE script you write at the beginning of each month. You must write it between the final day of a month (January 31, for example) and the third day of the new month (in our sample, this would be February 3). You *can* start this in the middle of a month or on any day, but if you plan to keep this as a regular routine, keep in mind that once you start the First of the Month Script on, say, the 11th (or whenever) of a month, *you must keep that as your "first day of the month"*—always.

Similar to other scripting, you write a journal entry as if it's the end of the month. Talk about how awesome [fill-in-the-blank month] was in detail. This is a really great way to have some fun with how far you can push your imagination, but it's important to stay more general with the First of the Month Script.

You only have one page to write, so focus on emotions—how you feel, how you want others to feel: "It was such a great month! I'm feeling so happy and excited! I love seeing my girlfriend so excited about the future." However, in addition to being general and focusing on emotion, it's important to add about three to five things from your Want Lists of the previous few weeks (*that could realistically occur within the next thirty days*), while not going into *too* much detail: "The middle of the month was amazing. I finally got the call I have been waiting for . . . they offered me the job! I also found the perfect puppy at the shelter, and she is fabulous."

Then you can add the bigger things that you could reasonably see happening in the coming thirty days. This is similar to what we talked about earlier—there is a power of adding things you *know* (or are pretty darn sure) will happen. Maybe you've wanted to lose a few pounds for a while, but not much has worked. If you know that you can lose five pounds in the span of four weeks (versus dangerously losing it in ten days), and that is your intention, this would be a good thing to include. Maybe you have seen great results with scripting and have been asking for an extra $10,000 to pay for a vacation for your sweetheart and you. If you believe it can happen within the month, put that down!

I don't do this every month, but I have taught friends this exercise and many have chosen to do it every month. This type of script is flexible and fun! I think everyone should try it at least once to see what happens. I have also found it helpful to journal an extra page on the last day of a month because it reinforces the good habit we have set up with our Daily Script and Nightly Journal. It's also really fun to see how much the First of the Month Script lines up with a Last of the Month Journal. Again, all of this is optional, but it comes in handy for our secret weapon: the Picture Script. More on that in a moment . . .

The Season Script

I love this one! The Season Script is exactly what it sounds like: scripting for the season ahead. For instance, if it's winter, you're scripting for spring. This is always a lot of fun because it allows us to select the things we love about each season. I don't care if you're a grinch; there is always something you can find to be excited for as each season approaches. Maybe it's something simple yet beautiful, like the smell of crisp autumn air. Maybe it's a family tradition like an annual beach trip every August.

If you're having trouble finding things you love about a certain season, pull out your scripting notebook and make a list. You might be surprised at what you write! I don't put a set time on the season script—what defines a season differs all around the world. You don't have to follow the equinox calendar or anything like that (though you can, of course).

This script could also be called a "Three-Month Script," because that is exactly what you are scripting ahead for. Maybe you are really excited about a vacation to Hawaii this summer that you've been planning for more than a year. Add that into the script! This script is great for looking at some of those longer term goals on your Daily Want List we talked about in the first few chapters (the kind that don't change every day). This script is about two to three pages MAX and follows the same format as the First of the Month Script.

If it is the end of winter, and you are about to do the Season Script for spring, you are going to pretend it is either the very end of summer or very beginning of autumn. You do this because it creates a loop and a pattern. You want to write this script as if you were writing it on the same day you would start your next Season Script. So, using our example, you want to imagine writing this script at the end of summer or beginning of fall for the "previous" spring. You can even include a few small details noting the season changing or something like Halloween coming up—it really is up to you.

Again, I would recommend doing an End of the Season Journal entry to see how well it matches up with the Season Script. It's amazing to see how incredibly lined up these become the more you practice.

New Year Script

You are very intelligent, so I think you get the picture! This follows the same formula as the Season Script and your First of the Month Script—except it is for the entire year! I would recommend that you don't do this one until you've been scripting for a few weeks or months and really have the hang of scripting. But, then again, I've had people *start* their scripting journey with this exercise and have great success.

The cool thing about the New Year Script is that it doesn't have to actually be the end of a year or the first of a new year. Any day can be the beginning of a new year for you. Some people (including me) like to do their New Year Script on their birthday. Either way, this script can be as short or long as you want! It can be one page or twenty. I wouldn't stress about it. Just have fun and try to include all of the things you want to see manifest in your life over the next year.

This script is powerful, and it creates so many positive memes. It also acts as a baseline for some people—something to refer back to if they ever feel stuck in the morning routine or Ten-Day Script. A little extra tip: do a fifty- to a hundred-item Want List before you do this script. People have reported all sorts of magic when they combine these two exercises. I also recommend doing an End of the Year Journal (whatever date the end of the year is for you) and compare.

◎ Creating a Picture Script

Okay, so you have been scripting for at least two weeks, and you have been doing your Ten-Day Script every Sunday (or whichever day you chose) and keeping up with your Daily Want List and Daily Belief List, and so on. Now you can dive into creating the crown jewel of scripting exercises: the Picture Script. Here's how:

Step 1: Obtain Your Poster Board

First you are going to obtain some sheets of poster board—dollar stores and pharmacies usually sell them. Don't overthink this: you can get fancy-colored ones or plain white ones. It really doesn't matter.

Step 2: Choose Your Base Script

Now you need to decide if you are going to use your Ten-Day Script or one of the above-mentioned scripts (First of the Month, Season, or New Year) as a base for the Picture Script. Some people hear about the Picture Script from me and decide they want to write one of the optional scripts first. If so, awesome! The beauty of the Picture Script is that using your Ten-Day Script is just as effective. So choose which of the "long" scripts you want to use as your base.

Step 3: Write an Outline

Now comes the fun part. To illustrate how this process works, let's say you are using your Ten-Day Script as your base and that you just wrote it last night. It just so happens that you are going to Hawaii in a few days and that you also just interviewed for a great job at an awesome public relations firm. You are single, and one of the Daily Want intentions you have been writing lately is that you intend to meet the perfect partner . . . and you live in Cleveland. First you are going to write out an outline of your next one to two weeks, using your most recent Ten-Day Script as a base. This is really simple and should take about five minutes. Include what you know will happen and what you want to create/manifest. Here is what it might look like:

Picture Script Outline

1. Pack for Hawaii.
2. Go to the airport.
3. Arrive in Kona.
4. Check in to a hotel.
5. Tour the area.
6. Take a volcano tour.
7. Receive a call from ACME Public Relations.
8. Get offered the job.
9. Go to a bar to celebrate.
10. Meet a gorgeous guy (he only lives an hour from me!).
11. Receive an email with details and contracts for new job.

12. Fly home.
13. Celebrate with friends at a favorite bar.
14. Start new job at ACME Public Relations.

Step 4: Create Your Memes

This is where we are going to focus on the memes and take a very different direction from the normal vision board. Go online or grab some magazines (online is way better!) and also grab your phone (or whatever you use to take photos). Now ask yourself the following questions:

What suitcase am I going to use?
How am I getting to the airport (SuperShuttle, bus, car, taxi)?
What airport am I flying out of?
What airline am I flying on?
What do the inside of the planes I'm flying on look like?
What kind of food do they serve?
What is the name of the airport in Kona I fly into?
How am I getting to my hotel?
What will I pass on the way to my hotel?
What hotel am I staying at?
What does the front desk of my hotel look like?
What tour company am I using to visit the volcano? (If you don't know yet, search for a few options of tour companies that provide these tours.)
What does the logo for the public relations firm look like?
Are there pictures online of the person who would call me to offer me the job?
What actors or people look like my dream mate?
What activities does my dream mate like to do?
How am I getting back home?
What do I wear on my first day of work?

This is where memes come in, and also where you begin to manifest using methods that work much better than taping abstract photos on a piece of poster board! Find photos online to represent the questions above and print them out and/or take a photo yourself.

What suitcase am I going to use? Take a photo of your suitcase, on your bed (or wherever you normally put your suitcase to pack it for a vacation). If you can, set up your camera to take a photo of you pretending to pack! (The more you put yourself into your Picture Script, the better.)

How am I getting to the airport (SuperShuttle, bus, car, taxi)? Find some pictures of a SuperShuttle or a taxi. If your friend is driving you, Google a picture of the type of car they drive and print that out. If you are driving your own car, print out a photo of your car.

What airport am I flying out of? Print a picture of the outside of the airport. There are plenty available on Google's image search or on the airport's official website. If you can't find a photo of the gate or outside of the airport, print one of the airport's logo.

What airline am I flying on? Print a photo of the airline's logo and have some fun with it. Sometimes I find stock photos of gate agents for the airline.

What do the inside of the planes I'm flying on look like? Let's say you are flying Hawaiian Airlines! Print some photos of their logo, their planes, etc.

What kind of food do they serve? Google pictures of the delicious food trays they serve on Hawaiian Airlines.

What is the name of the airport in Kona I fly into? Print some photos of the airport in Kona and maybe even the baggage area where you pick up your bags.

How am I getting to my hotel? Print a photo of the shuttle or taxi or, if you're renting a car, print a photo of the rental company's logo.

What will I pass on the way to my hotel? This is a secret trick to really script using pictures in timeline form. Look up the local grocery stores and shops. When I was doing a similar board back in 2016 using my Season Script, I didn't even have any way of getting to Hawaii, but I found pictures of Foodland, the local grocery chain on the Big Island, and printed pictures of the outside and inside. It's the small, but significant details like this that are part of the magic of the Picture Script! I ended up vacationing in Hawaii a few months later.

What hotel am I staying at? Have fun with this. Print out photos of the hotel logo, the outside of the hotel, the surrounding restaurants, etc.

What does the front desk of my hotel look like? Print a photo of the front desk or check-in area. Most hotels have this on their website, but if not, use a stock photo and tape a small logo of the hotel above the front-desk people in the photo.

What tour company am I using to visit the volcano? If you don't know yet, search for a few options of tour companies that provide these tours. Print photos of the tour-company logo, their vehicles if they have them, and pictures of what you want to see on your tour.

What does the logo for the public relations firm look like? Print out the logo. A photo of the building wouldn't work in this spot on the board, but it will at the end.

Are there pictures online of the person who would call me to offer me the job? If so, print out a photo of them. If not, look for stock photos using search terms like "two women on the phone" or "business-women shaking hands," anything to evoke the image of you getting the job. Also, get a picture of yourself and cut out your head and paste it onto the body of one of the women. To some this may sound crazy, but your subconscious understands photos, and this is a direct message to it! (More on this below.) If this makes you feel weird, take a photo of yourself on a phone and use that with a stock photo of someone on the phone who looks like they might work at the firm.

What actors or people look like my dream mate? This is easy. Print out some photos of people who evoke the feeling of your perfect mate. They don't have to be famous; just do some Google searching. Maybe you want your mate to have the sense of humor of Robin Williams and the looks of Brad Pitt. If so, print out pictures of them. Print out some hearts or any symbols that make you think of new love as well.

What activities does my dream mate like to do? You want some images of couples in Hawaii doing activities (snorkeling, scuba diving, sitting at a bar, etc.) that you would love to do with your new mate. This is another great opportunity to add yourself into the picture!

How am I getting back home? The idea here is that you have a few printed photos that represent the plane ride back home and arriving home happy.

What do I wear on my first day of work? If you already know which outfit you would wear on the first day of your new job at ACME Public Relations, awesome! Take a photo of yourself in the outfit smiling! Or take a photo of the clothes laid out on your bed. If you don't have an outfit picked out, then go online and find a photo of the outfit you want. Or you can just print a picture of someone wearing an outfit you love and tape a picture of your head onto their body!

Here's the thing: **you're gonna want a lot of photos of your head—** some smiling facing forward and some smiling from the side (left and right profile) so that you can paste them over the heads of people in stock photos. This may sound strange, but I promise you, it makes this process incredibly more powerful. I'll give you a quick personal example. Solly and I were struggling to lose some major weight we had gained—more than seventy pounds each. While we were able to use normal scripting to help us lose about twenty pounds, it wasn't until we started looking at pictures of guys with bodies that we felt were near what we wanted to look like and put them up on Picture Script boards with our heads on those bodies that we were able to see some real progress. Within a six-month period, I lost fifty-two pounds, and Solly lost forty-two. This also is a result of our ExtraCom System pointing out ways to be the vision of the person we saw on the Picture Script board.

When you communicate to your subconscious in a language it understands on a primal level (pictures), it allows your subconscious to absorb that new meme. That meme is a computer program, which helps you to do your morning routine and also helps guide your scripting, which in turn leads to action. The memes inspired us to eat better, work out, and so on.

The process for creating these photos is really, really low tech. You don't need Photoshop. In fact there is an incredible FREE website called ImageChef where you can make some amazing pictures for your Picture Script. It's very low tech and user friendly. My sixty-five-year-old dad uses it for his Picture Scripts easily—and he is the most low-tech person I know! A simple internet search will lead to many sites like this. Some of the things you can make on these sites and then include on your Picture Script

*Fig. 10.1. A variety of sample Picture Script
photos created on ImageChef*

include mock-up business cards or badges showing your new job at your dream company, movie marquees shining your name in lights, strategies for advertising your bestselling book, and signs advertising you as a famous speaker—or maybe even as a presidential hopeful!

If you prefer even lower tech, get crafty and make your own memes using magazine cutouts. I make my pictures in either Microsoft Word or Apple Pages. It's actually really easy. Let's say I am helping my sister-in-law, Tiffany, make a Picture Script using the example above (Hawaii, new job, new guy). First I pull up a blank document in landscape mode (the wide one) and set my font size to something insane, like 500. I then press enter (the cursor is as big as each page, so I'm making lots of blank pages by pressing enter on a 500-point font). Then I go and grab the photos I need. So, for instance, if I am helping Tiffany make her Picture Script, we need a photo of her packing a suitcase. She doesn't have one, so I find these photos on Google by searching "girl packing suitcase."

Now I pick one of these photos and then find a photo of Tiffany where her head could be matched up easily onto the head of the girl in the photo. If Tiffany and I can't find a photo of her head that works, I would just have her take one of herself. So Tiffany and I find this photo of Tiffany with her best friend, Barb.

Fig. 10.2. Barb and Tiffany

We play around with it by eyeballing the size of Tiffany's head and fig-uring out what size would look best when we print out the photos for our Picture Script. (Word and Pages allow you to size photos with the drag of a mouse.) Once we have all the photos we need (anywhere from eight to fifteen pages), and we feel pretty good, Tiff and I put the photos next to each other on the document and we print! Then we grab our handy scissors and tape.

Solly uses a program on his iPad that is similar to Photoshop. I have no idea how to use it, but if you do, then by all means, use it to create the finished photos ahead of time before you print. But if you're like me, you would print, then cut out Tiffany's head like this:

Fig. 10.3. Cutout of Tiffany's head

Then we tape the cutout over the stock photo we found online of the woman packing her suitcase like this:

Fig. 10.4. Tiffany with packed suitcase

You can do this with lots of the pictures on your Picture Script! Take a look below and at the photos on pages 188 and 189. You can also print and tape some words or phrases on the photo to give it some extra punch (more on this in step 5).

Fig. 10.5. Creating a celebrating Tiffany photo

"I got the job at Acme Public Relations!!"

Fig. 10.6. Celebrating Tiffany photo with word overlay

Remember, when it comes to cutting and pasting your head onto pictures you've printed, it does NOT have to be perfect. If the person in the original photo has hair that sticks out over yours, don't stress. The important thing here is that the photo for the Picture Script makes you feel things: love, happiness, contentment, relief, and so on. And, don't forget, images that represent things in your Picture Script flow chart (see page 191) are just as powerful and important.

You want to have a good balance here of pictures that evoke what you

Fig. 10.7. Stock image of man and woman

Fig. 10.8. Tiffany with potential dream mate

want to feel (some with you in them and some without you) and ones that represent the time line you are scripting out for yourself (the airport, hotel, etc.). You are doing the same thing with the Picture Script that you do with your normal script: using real things you know are going to happen and adding in the things you are manifesting to select and bring into your reality a new love, job, etc.

Fig. 10.9. Stock image of women shaking hands

Fig. 10.10. Tiffany shaking hands with potential PR employer

Step 5: Add Words and Phrases

It is really important that you include a few words and phrases—ideally ones that sum up the intents from your Daily Want List that you are using on your Picture Script. For this example, words like "I got the job!" "Love," and "Paradise" are great. Another fun thing you can do if you are creating a picture meme with you and, say, the person calling you to tell you that you got the job, is to print out some short lines of text and post them over the photo like the example of Tiffany celebrating in the image on page 187. These words and phrases are extremely powerful. They help align the worlds of memetics and scripting/New Thought. Together with

Fig. 10.11. Photos representing love

the photos, the words drive a direct command not only into your sub-conscious center of creation but also out into the Nexus, which is like a computer command that makes you select (a.k.a. manifest) this reality into your existence.

Step 6: Decide on a Direction for Your Photos

Okay, this next part is crucial. You are going to look at your blank poster board and pick a direction for the pictures. What do I mean? Well, one of the big things that makes the Picture Script so different is that you are scripting using photos to tell your story of how you want things to be as if they have already occurred, using pictures of things that have "already hap-

A

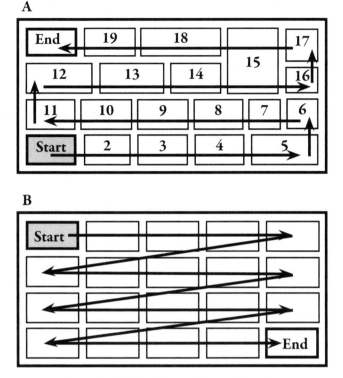

B

Fig. 10.12. Two Picture Script flow charts

pened," and you are creating these images with your own picture/head in the photo. The VERY important part here is that you take a look at the little outline that you did in step 3 and choose the direction you want your pictures to go. It isn't really important where on the board you choose to start, but it is important that you keep the pictures in the order of your outline. Above are a couple of images to show you some ideas of where you could place your first picture and how the others could flow from there.

Step 7: Create Your Picture Script

Really, you can start in any corner. The above illustrations show just two of a few ways you can do this. As long as YOU know that it makes sense, chronologically, then you will be just fine. Next tape all the photos onto your poster board in chronological order of how you are scripting them to play out (remember, we are using your Ten-Day Script as a guide for this

Fig. 10.13. Tiffany's Picture Script

example). So in either box above where it says "start," you would put the photo of your suitcase and in the square to the right of start can be either the photo of you packing it or a photo or photos that represent the way you get to the airport.

Please don't be rigid about how many photos you have! You need at least one for each section of the Picture Script, but I always have a few subjects (for instance if I am really excited about the airplane food or the hotel pool) where I have a few photos to represent each part of the script. Also, you don't have to use every photo! You may alter your original flow chart slightly too. I personally don't like empty space on my Picture Script, so I like to fit as much in as possible, while keeping it in chronological order.

Using our example and my lovely sister-in-law, Tiffany, here is an idea of what this Picture Script might look like, with our time line beginning at the top upper left corner.

Step 8. Display Your Picture Script

Now hang it up! You don't have to put it in your living room where the whole world can see it. Some people tape it to the inside of their closet door. It is important that you look at it, however, and if you do have a place where you can see it regularly, even peripherally, that is great! I just don't want you to stress if you don't have a space for it, because much of the magic is in the action of creating the Picture Script itself!

I want to add a few things that are really, really important here. It is 100 percent okay to have more than one Picture Script hanging up at a time! Sometimes I make one every day to represent a different aspect of what I am working on, or "selecting from the Nexus" (manifesting). Sometimes I do three in one day, so I hang those up with any other ones I've recently done. Don't be afraid to make more than one in a short period of time.

Also, don't be afraid to recycle and use the other blank side for your next Picture Script. Some people like to tape two blank ones together (I do this quite often) because they need more room. When you have totally used up both sides and feel like the Picture Script's time is done, just recycle it or throw it away. There is literally no need for you to hang on to old boards.

There will, of course, be days and weeks when you have zero Picture

Scripts hanging up—and that's okay too! *That is the beauty of scripting: you make it work for you, not the other way around.* The possibilities for what you put on the Picture Script are literally endless—just like the possibilities that scripting gives you.

Remember what we talked about in chapter 3? You have to be brave enough to admit to yourself what it is that you want. It's okay to be "selfish" . . . a horrible word often used by jealous people who can't see the power of self-love and self-empowerment. I'm not saying that truly selfish, evil people don't exist in the world. They do. But they don't have to be a part of our reality. Good people need to understand that it is okay to want and dream. YOU need to understand this. Many times a person will tell you that you are selfish for pursuing your dreams, and yet many of those fulfilled dreams end up helping and/or empowering many more people than you ever could have imagined. Ironically, this often includes the person who originally called you selfish.

EVERYONE LOVES A TWIST ENDING

The marvelous is everywhere. In things it appears as soon as one succeeds in penetrating any object whatever. The most humble of them, just by itself, raises every issue. Its form, which reveals its individual structure, is the result of transformations which have been going on since the world began. And it contains the germs of countless possibilities that will be realized in the future.

The marvelous is also between all things and all beings, interpenetrating space, where our senses perceive nothing directly; but the space is filled with energy, waves and forces in continual motion, where equilibrium is achieved for a moment, where all the transformations are in preparation. Far from being independent isolated units, objects are part of compositions, huge fragile assemblies or solid constructs, realities that the eyes perceive only as fragments but that the mind conceives as whole.

PIERRE MABILLE, *MIRROR OF THE MARVELOUS*

Dare to push yourself to script what it is you truly want. Write the story you want to see, from having a good day—every day—to finally experiencing what you have always imagined for yourself and your life. Scripting is, by its very nature and process, a very private experience. You don't have to tell a soul what you are up to when they start asking why things seem to suddenly be going so well for you. They *will* ask, because a person who uses scripting is a person living their life to the fullest, and that can be seen and sensed by others. But you don't have to tell a soul if you don't want to—this is your journey and yours alone. A journey for which to be grateful.

My friend Mitch Horowitz gave me a gift the first time we ever met in person. We had been friends online for years, but when the day finally came to meet in person, he was giving a talk to a group of people in New York City. After the talk, he handed me and the others a little red book called *It Works,* which Mitch talked about earlier in the foreword. At the end of this awesome little book is a piece of advice, which I wish to now pass on to you:

> You can have what you want but you must take all that goes with it: so in planning your wants, plan that which you are sure will give to you and your fellow man the greatest good here on earth; thus paving the way to that future hope beyond the pale of human understanding.
>
> Many worthwhile desires will find their place on your list. One will be to help others as you have been helped. Great is the reward to those who help and give without thought of self as it is impossible to be unselfish without gain.[1]

I can't quite ever truly express in words the endless depths of gratitude I have for Mitch. He not only gave me the idea for this book *and* urged me to write it, he also wrote the foreword for it.

Here's a little secret that I alluded to in the introduction: *Mitch Horowitz scripted this book into existence.* We both did, actually, but Mitch was the match that lit the fuse of something I had been writing in my Daily Want List for a little more than a year, and he didn't even know it.

One of my dreams and intentions was to receive a multibook deal. I had been writing this intent and scripting about it casually for well over a year, trusting that it would somehow happen. The thing is, I had only written *one* book and had assumed that book would lead to a contract for more books. I told no one about any of this. Then Mitch called me one day sounding more excited than I had ever heard him. He had recently started using my little scripting method and was having great results. I was thrilled for him. He told me that I immediately needed to write a book on scripting. I was humbled, but also a little scared: *Could I write an entire book on scripting?*

Mitch was so confident that I could write this book that he told me he was going to write the foreword for it as soon as we hung up from the phone call. Usually the foreword is the *last* piece of a book's journey, written long after the final manuscript is completed. Despite this, Mitch wrote the most amazing, kind words and sent them to me an hour after we had hung up the phone. *I now had a foreword to a book that I hadn't written yet.* It existed; it just hadn't been selected and pulled out of the Nexus into our physical world yet. So I got right to work doing *my* part of scripting it into being. On page 197 is my final Picture Script for this very book.

This is an amazing instance of two people's scripts and intentions coming together. Mitch's script was the foreword (itself an affirmation of a completed project), which aligned with the deal I had myself been intending and scripting to bring into my reality for a long time. Up until that moment, I had only *one* book being reviewed by publishers! I now had a path to bring my heart's dream, my intention of having multiple books published, into reality.

So if you had any lingering doubts about whether scripting works . . . you are literally holding in your hands a script and the result of a script brought into reality.

Now THAT is something to write about.

*Fig. 10.14.
Picture
Script for
Scripting
the Life
You Want*

Acknowledgments

I COULD FILL AN ENTIRE BOOK with the names of those whom I have never-ending gratitude to for being a part of the journey that led to this book being brought into this world.

All of my teachers and educators from Marlton, New Jersey, who believed in me and gave me the self-confidence to follow my passions: Ms. Elaine Winder, Mrs. Nicole Snodgrass, Mrs. Carol Smith, Mr. Scott Powell, Ms. Colleen Peelman, Mr. Frank Guerrini, Mr. Scott Sax, Mrs. Marilyn Sobeleski, Ms. Barron, Mrs. Lance, and the many others from Marlton Elementary School, Marlton Middle School, and Cherokee High School who are too numerous to name, I thank you all for encouraging me and helping me unearth my passion for writing and the arts.

Mitch Horowitz for his guidance and help making this book real.

The team at Inner Traditions for your friendship and the fun: Jennie Marx, Manzanita Carpenter-Sanz, Jon Graham, John Hays, Patricia Rydle, Kelly Bowen, Erica B. Robinson, Jeanie Levitan, Megan Rule, and Ehud Sperling.

My first spiritual mentor, Jeffrey Sean Poole, I miss you every single day.

My dad, Frank, for allowing and encouraging me to always walk my own path and supporting me no matter where it led. My father-in-law, Mike Hemus, for being not only the best dad to my Solly, but for being my friend. I'm grateful for you both.

Jerry and Esther Hicks and their teachings of Abraham, for guiding me from afar since I was sixteen years old.

My cousins, Mallory, Audra, Pamela, Brittany, Melissa, and Amanda.

Teddi Alvarez and Lori Olsen for being the best hair and nail team, and Walid Azami for being such a phenomenally talented photographer and shooting the campaign for this book.

Oliva Mah, Dorian Newberry, and Karen Crietz for making friendship so fun and easy.

Adriane Schwartz, who will yell at me for saying this, but I'm going to anyway: for coming in at the perfect time in my life and showing me that not only can I write but that I also love to write. Your mentorship and guidance built me back up at a time when I needed it most. You're the best and I love you. If not for you, none of this would have happened. Thank you from the bottom of my heart.

I'm going to forget some names, and I apologize, but I also wish to thank: Thea De Sousa, Liz Pryor, Mary Jo Eustace, Sally Kirkland, Leslee and Robin Godshalk, Ashlee Godshalk Ruggles, Tamara Godshalk, Sandi DiMarco, Alan Grayson, Melissa Jo Peltier, John Gray, Jen Kirkman, Tony Serrata, Luli Batista, Tracey Michaels, Steven Hemus-Lance, Tristan and Niko Pappas, Brandon Camacho, Ryan Daly, Mara Santino, Nils Larsen, Stella Alex, Mark Smith, Tasha Smith, Natalie Carson, Brian Carson, Valerie Hartford, Stacey Sanderson, Gary Swartzman, Uncle Bob Swartzman, Michelle and Joel Pardini, the Swartzman Family, the Hemus Family, Bob McFadden, Billy McFadden, Billy McFadden Jr., Nikki McFadden, Ella McFadden, Cathi McFadden, Melissa Whittenweiler, Brit Morgan, Barbara Whitson, Ashlei Sobrero, Pete Sobrero, Kayla Hansen, Amanda Quintor, Lori Osborne, Tiffany Champlin, Jim Lefter, Harv Bishop, Opal Vadhan, and Gabriel.

Notes

CHAPTER 1.
EXCUSE ME, YOUR LIFE IS WAITING

1. Mitch Horowitz, *The Miracle Club* (Rochester, Vt.: Inner Traditions, 2018), 109.

CHAPTER 2. SCARY, TERRIFYING MIRACLES

1. George W. Meek, *From Enigma to Science* (New York: Samuel Weiser, Inc., 1977).
2. Lynn Grabhorn, *Excuse Me, Your Life Is Waiting* (Charlottesville, Va.: Hampton Roads Publishing Company, 1999), 12.

CHAPTER 3.
STEP ONE: WRITE YOUR DAILY WANT LIST

1. Mitch Horowitz, *The Miracle of a Definite Chief Aim* (New York: Gildan Media Corp., 2017), xii–xiii.
2. Tim Knight, "The Power of Belief," *The Focus 3 Blog*, posted June 11, 2019.
3. Wikipedia, "reticular formation," section 3.1, "ascending reticular activating system."
4. Akshay Gupta, "How Your Brain's Reticular Activating System (RAS) determines Your Success," Fearless Motivation (website), posted October 16, 2017.
5. Kate Kershner, "What's the Baader-Meinhof Phenomenon?" How Stuff Works (website).
6. Pacific Standard Staff, "There's a Name for That: The Baader-Meinhoff Phenomenon," Pacific Standard (website), posted June 14, 2017.

7. "The No. 1 Habit Billionaires Run Daily" (YouTube video), posted by Be Inspired on February 12, 2019.

8. Gupta, "How Your Brain's Reticular Activating System (RAS) determines Your Success."

9. "The No. 1 Habit Billionaires Run Daily" (YouTube video).

CHAPTER 6. UM . . . WHY DOES THIS WORK?

1. Lisa Zyga, "Physicists Provide Support for Retrocausal Quantum Theory in Which the Future Influences the Past," Phys.org, July 5, 2017.

2. Laura G. Williams, Tal Linzen, David Poeppel, and Alec Marantz, "In Spoken Word Recognition, the Future Predicts the Past," *Journal of Neuroscience* 38, no. 35 (August 29, 2018), Journal of Neuroscience website.

3. "Reality Doesn't Exist Until We Measure It: Quantum Experiment Confirms," *Cosmic Scientist* (blog), May 6, 2016.

4. "Is Our World a Simulation? Why Some Scientists Say It's More Likely Than Not," *Guardian* (website).

5. Dick Pelletier, "Parallel Worlds Exist and Will Soon Be Testable, Expert Says," *Mind Unleashed* (website), January 16, 2014.

6. Clara Moskowitz, "Are We Living in a Computer Simulation?," *Scientific American* (website), April 7, 2016.

7. Robert Coolman, "What Is Quantum Mechanics?," Live Science (website), September 26, 2014.

8. Wikipedia, "many-worlds interpretation."

9. Wikipedia, "Copenhagen interpretation."

10. Wikipedia, "Schrödinger's cat."

11. Weizmann Institute of Science, "Quantum Theory Demonstrated: Observation Affects Reality," ScienceDaily (website), February 27, 1998.

12. Jesse Emspak, "Quantum Entanglement: Love on a Subatomic Scale," Space .com, February 14, 2016.

13. Matthew Leifer, "Does Time-Symmetry in Quantum Theory Imply Retrocausality?" (Orange, Calif.: Chapman University, 2016).

14. Matthew Leifer and Matthew Pusey, "Is a Time Symmetric Interpretation of Quantum Theory Possible without Retrocausality?," Royal Society Publishing (website), June 21, 2017.

15. Paul Ratner, "A New Quantum Theory Predicts That the Future Could Be Influencing the Past," Big Think (website), July 9, 2017.

16. A. G. Manning, R. I. Khakimov, R. G. Dall, and A. G. Truscott, "Wheeler's Delayed-Choice Gedanken Experiment with a Single Atom," *Nature* (website), May 25, 2015.

17. "Experiment Confirms Quantum Theory Weirdness," Australian National University website, May 27, 2015.

18. Williams, "In Spoken Word Recognition," *Journal of Neuroscience,* 7585–99.

19. Robbert Dijkgraaf, "There Are No Laws of Physics. There's Only the Landscape," Quanta Magazine (website), June 4, 2018.

20. Dijkgraaf, "There Are No Laws of Physics."

21. Dijkgraaf, "There Are No Laws of Physics."

22. Anil Ananthaswamy, "A New Quantum Paradox Flags Errors in Our View of Reality," *Wired* (website), December 9, 2018.

23. Ananthaswamy, "A New Quantum Paradox Flags Errors in Our View of Reality."

24. Ananthaswamy, "A New Quantum Paradox Flags Errors in Our View of Reality."

25. Ananthaswamy, "A New Quantum Paradox Flags Errors in Our View of Reality."

26. Ananthaswamy, "A New Quantum Paradox Flags Errors in Our View of Reality."

27. Kristie Miller, "The Block Universe Theory, Where Time Travel Is Possible but Time Passing Is an Illusion," ABC website (News/Science page), September 1, 2018.

28. Miller, "The Block Universe Theory."

29. Rachel Thomas, "The Future Is Time," Plus Magazine (website), September 30, 2016.

30. Wikipedia, "determinism."

CHAPTER 7.
SELECTING THE NEXUS, OR
HOW TO BREAK OUT OF THE SIMULATION FOR $0

1. simon_2112, "I know now that I don't exist," Glitch in the Matrix forum, Reddit, posted January 17, 2014.

2. simon_2112, "I know now that I don't exist."

3. Neurotrace, "Died on the corner," Glitch in the Matrix forum, Reddit, posted October 8, 2012.

4. ScreamWax, "I literally died—or so I thought," Glitch in the Matrix forum, Reddit, posted November 26, 2017.

5. boruxzetto, "This isn't my apartment?" Glitch in the Matrix forum, Reddit, posted December 25, 2017.

6. thistlegirl, "It's part of the reason we bought the house," Glitch in the Matrix forum, Reddit, posted March 22, 2017.

7. WholyFunny, "Cool, simple glitch?" Glitch in the Matrix forum, Reddit, posted September 19, 2015.

8. oedipal, "Jewelry glitch," Glitch in the Matrix forum, Reddit, posted May 28, 2018.

9. Walter Russell, *The Universal One* (Waynesboro, Va.: The University of Science and Philosophy, 1974), 9.

10. Olivia Solon, "Is Our World a Simulation? Why Some Scientists Say It's More Likely Than Not," *Guardian* (website), posted October 11, 2016.

11. Nick Bostrom, "Do We Live in a Computer Simulation?" *New Scientist,* 192, no. 2579 (November 19, 2006), 38–39. Can be found on the Simulation Argument website.

12. Nick Bostrom, "The Simulation Argument FAQ," The Simulation Argument (website), updated 2011.

13. Solon, "Is Our World a Simulation?"

14. Solon, "Is Our World a Simulation?"

15. Graham Templeton, "Neil deGrasse Tyson Says It's 'Very Likely' the Universe Is a Simulation," ExtremeTech (website), April 22, 2016.

16. "2016 Isaac Asimov Memorial Debate: Is the Universe a Simulation?" YouTube video.

17. Templeton, "Neil deGrasse Tyson Says It's 'Very Likely' the Universe Is a Simulation."

18. Templeton, "Neil deGrasse Tyson Says It's 'Very Likely' the Universe Is a Simulation."

19. Solon, "Is Our World a Simulation?"

20. Donald Hoffman, "Do We See Reality as It Is?" talk presented at an official TED conference, March 2015.

21. Hoffman, "Do We See Reality as It Is?"

22. Hoffman, "Do We See Reality as It Is?"

23. Hoffman, "Do We See Reality as It Is?"

24. Hoffman, "Do We See Reality as It Is?"

25. Hoffman, "Do We See Reality as It Is?"

26. Hoffman, "Do We See Reality as It Is?"
27. Hoffman, "Do We See Reality as It Is?"
28. Hoffman, "Do We See Reality as It Is?"
29. Hoffman, "Do We See Reality as It Is?"
30. "D-Wave," lecture by Geordie Rose, IdeaCity (YouTube video), posted by Saul Colquhoun, July 9, 2013.
31. "D-Wave," lecture by Geordie Rose.
32. "D-Wave," lecture by Geordie Rose.
33. Roey Tzezana, "Singularity: Explain It to Me Like I'm 5-Years-Old," Futurism (website), March 3, 2017.
34. Christianna Reedy, "Kurzweil Claims That the Singularity Will Happen by 2045," Futurism (website), October 5, 2017.
35. Reedy, "Kurzweil Claims That the Singularity Will Happen by 2045."
36. Matt Swayne, "Is a Spiritual Singularity Near?" Singularity Weblog, November 2, 2010.
37. Swayne, "Is a Spiritual Singularity Near?"
38. Reddit (website), "r/randonauts," home page.
39. "Chaos Game" (YouTube video), posted by Numberphile on April 27, 2017.
40. "Chaos Game" (YouTube video).
41. Reddit (website), "r/randonauts," theory page.
42. Reddit (website), "r/randonauts," theory page.
43. Reddit (website), "r/randonauts," theory page.
44. Reddit (website), "r/randonauts," FAQ page.
45. Mitch Horowitz, *The Miracle Club* (Rochester, Vt.: Inner Traditions, 2018), 153.
46. Telegraph reporters, "Professor Stephen Hawking's Final Theory: The Universe Is a Hologram," *Telegraph* (website), May 2, 2018.
47. Telegraph reporters, "Professor Stephen Hawking's Final Theory."
48. Telegraph reporters, "Professor Stephen Hawking's Final Theory."
49. Ian Steadman, "Cosmic Rays Offer Clue Our Universe Could Be a Computer Simulation," *Wired* (website), October 11, 2012.
50. Kristen Hileman, "Transformations of Esu," available on the Black Electorate website.

CHAPTER 8. PUTTING IT ALL TOGETHER

1. Lynn Grabhorn, *Excuse Me, Your Life Is Waiting* (Charlottesville, Va.: Hampton Roads Publishing Company, 1999), 175.

2. Richard Brodie, *Virus of the Mind* (Carlsbad, Calif.: Hay House, 1996), 28.
3. "The Health Benefits of Journaling," PsychCentral (website), last updated October 8, 2018.

CHAPTER 9. THE SWORD OF SCRIPTING

1. Richard Brodie, *Virus of the Mind* (Carlsbad, Calif.: Hay House, 1996), xvi.
2. Brodie, *Virus,* xviii.
3. Richard Dawkins, "Memes: The New Replicators" in *The Selfish Gene* (Oxford, U.K.: Oxford University Press, 1976), 192.
4. Dawkins, *Memes,* 192.
5. Brodie, *Virus,* xiv.
6. Aaron Lynch, *Thought Contagion* (New York: HarperCollins, 1996) 2.
7. Brodie, *Virus,* xviii.

CHAPTER 10. APEX CREATOR

1. R. H. J., *It Works* (New York: TarcherPerigee, 2016 [deluxe ed.]), 13.

Index

Page numbers in *italics* refer to illustrations.

Law of Attraction, 11, 23, 79
  like attracts like, 19–20
  and manifesting, 34
Leifer, Matthew, 93–94
life
  addressing your own life in a script,
    61–62
  difficulties in, 77–78
lobster in a dress shop, 15
Lynch, Aaron, 169

Mabille, Pierre, 194
magic, 15–16
  defined, 75–78
  of the mundane, 40–42
manifesting. *See also* scripting
  defined, 6, 34
  and feeling jazzed, 133
  Grabhorn's four basic steps, 17–18
  selection and, 132–36
many-worlds theory, 82–83
marvelous, the, 194
Matrix, The, 100
measuring, effect on outcome, 84–85
memes, 143–44, 159, 160–71
  defined, 161–62, 165–66
  how they come into existence, 166
  as missing key to manifesting, 161
memetics, 143, 162
Miller, Kristie, 95–97
mind, 165
  language of, 171–73
mind viruses, 143. *See also* memes
Miracle Club, The (Horowitz), xi, 14, 132
miracles, 15–16, 34
morning routine, 151–52, 156–58
M-theory, 91

mugging, author's experience of, 28–32
multiverse, 134–35
mundane, magic of the, 40–42
Murray, Bill, 17
Musk, Elon, 108, 118

natural selection, 110–15
negativity, not added to scripts, 142, 144
New Thought, xiii, 6, 13–15, 74–75,
    116, 134, 138, 170
  and creating in another's reality,
    165–66
  omissions in, 4
  and Royce Christyn's work, x–xi
  science and, 74–75
New Year Script, 177
Nexus, as point of connection, 136–38
Nightly Journal, 54–56, 142, 157–58
  examples of, 55, 57
notebook, writing script on, 147–51
noticing, 44. *See also* RAS (reticular
    activating system)

observer effect, 85–86
Occam's razor, 100, 105–6

paints and brushes analogy, 143
parallel universes, 82, 115–16, 120
past, influenced by the future, 87–90
perception, and reality, 110–15
permission, to be selfish, 32–34
Peter Pan List, 153–54
photos, for Picture Script, 180–89
physical objects changing, 104–6
pictures, as language of mind, 171–73
Picture Script, the, 174–94
  creating, 178–94